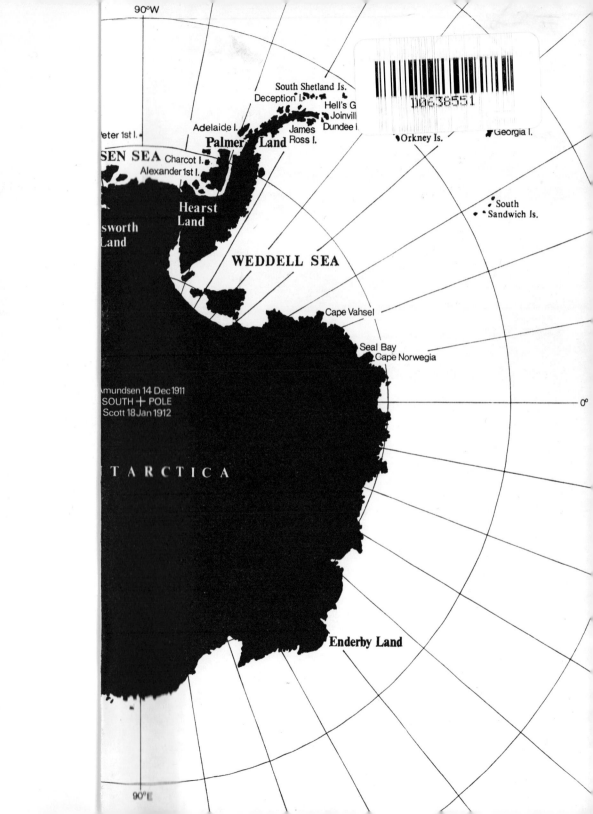

90°W

South Shetland Is.
Deception I.
Hell's G
Joinvill
Dundee I.
Adelaide I.
James
Ross I.
Palmer Land
eter 1st I.
Orkney Is.
Georgia I.
SEN SEA Charcot I.
Alexander 1st I.

South
Sandwich Is.

Hearst
Land

sworth
Land

WEDDELL SEA

Cape Vahsel

Seal Bay
Cape Norwegia

Amundsen 14 Dec 1911
SOUTH ✛ POLE
Scott 18 Jan 1912

0°

T A R C T I C A

Enderby Land

90°E

MAGNUS L. OLSEN

Saga of
the White
Horizon

Nautical Publishing Company Limited

© 1972 by MAGNUS L. OLSEN

ISBN 0 245 51079 6

First published in Great Britain in 1972 by

NAUTICAL PUBLISHING COMPANY

Nautical House, Lymington, Hampshire

*Composed in 11 on 12 pt Monotype Baskerville
and made and printed in Great Britain by*
THE CAMELOT PRESS LIMITED
LONDON AND SOUTHAMPTON

Contents

Illustrations

MAPS

CHAPTER ONE

Prelude to Adventure

I was nineteen years old when in March 1933, I passed my final examinations at the Norwegian Naval School at Horten, and became entitled to the rank of Sub-Lieutenant. Although I had been a Sea Cadet, my training had included flying, and during the winter months, I had to fit the plane with skis, in order to practise take off and landing on the ice of the frozen Oslofjord.

One day the Commanding Officer summoned me to his office, and asked me to take a gentleman in the plane with me, without informing me who my passenger was to be. I was instructed first to land on the ice in the fjord, and then on a field on which the snow had drifted. The second landing, needless to say, was extremely bumpy, but my passenger appeared to be quite unconcerned.

It was a great surprise to learn the following day that my passenger had been Rear-Admiral Byrd of the American Navy, who in 1929 had been the first explorer to take planes to the Antarctic. He was an expert pilot himself, but he had taken with him on that expedition a young Norwegian airman, Mr Bernt Balchen, who was later to become the head of the American Air Force.

As Admiral Byrd was then planning a second even greater expedition to the Antarctic that year, he had come to Norway to order equipment for it.

Another American, a very wealthy explorer named Mr Lincoln Ellsworth, was at that time planning an expedition of his own to the Antarctic. His ambition was mainly to fly right across the vast Southern Continent, and he had already asked Mr Bernt Balchen to go with him, owing to his previous experience with the Byrd Expedition. But a young second pilot was necessary to be on hand in emergency, so Rear-Admiral

Byrd had been asked to select one for Mr Ellsworth while he was in Norway.

I was speechless to learn that I had been chosen to be that second pilot, particularly since the selection had been made by Rear-Admiral Byrd in consultation with my Commanding Officer. I had not even recognized my passenger, nor guessed the purpose of his coming in the tiny plane with me.

That evening, on returning to my lodgings, I kept wondering why I was the one to be chosen. My mind travelled back to my childhood days to find the explanation. What were the qualities necessary to stand up to the unknown hazards of the Antarctic? I had to go very deep into my memories to find the answer.

Firstly, I was the son of a sea captain who never sailed without his wife, and even as a baby I had been handed over to my great-grandparents to be looked after. My great-grandfather, Anders Olsen, had been one of the first captains on the Fred Olsen Line ships, and although he had retired long before I was born, he could never leave the sea, and had bought a fishing-cutter to occupy his time.

My earliest memory of the boat was from my position on the side in the wheel-house. The old man had removed the legs from a dark green chair, which he had then screwed to the side. Before setting out on a fishing trip he strapped me into it. From this elevated position, I had an excellent view of the sea, as there were windows all round. Indeed, the sea became more familiar to me than the streets, the garden, or even the walls of my great-grandfather's house, which was built at the outer part of the Larvikfjord.

My recollections of my great-grandmother are hazy, but I do remember her dressing me to go to the dairy each morning to collect the milk in the wintertime, when the fjord was frozen and we could not go fishing. I had a bright red woollen cap and mittens to match, but once out of my great-grandmother's sight, these were stuffed up my jersey. My hands *had* to be bare!

One trick which I had learned to perform at an early age was to raise myself to a horizontal position by holding on to a pole. The news of this achievement got around our little community, and one day a man drew me aside and asked to see my trick. There was no pole but he held out a branch vertically for me. I agreed to perform only if he paid me 2 öre. Laughing, the man promised to pay my fee, and he even gave me 10 öre for my effort.

I had learned this acrobatic feat on the boat quite accidentally. In rough weather, it pitched and rolled, and as soon as I had graduated from my wall chair, and could move about the ship, I had to grab the rails which lead to the wheel-house, many times, in order to keep my balance. In doing so, I discovered that I could project myself horizontally, and when I returned home with my great-grandfather, I practised my art on dry land.

Sometimes I visited my mother's parents, Bestefar and Bestemor Carlsen. Grandpa Carlsen had been a seafarer as well, as a chief steward on a large sailing ship. On their sitting-room table stood a great model of this ship, and I loved to stand and gaze up at it. I wanted so much to feel it and play with the rigging, but it was much too high for me, although I was able to reach up and stroke the hull.

Before my great-grandfather died, he had introduced me to the mysteries of the compass, as well as teaching me to read a little from the Bible which he always carried on the boat. Every day before we set out on a trip, he read me a chapter, and another when we returned after he had moored the boat beside our little pier. In some ways therefore I was a little precocious, as Norwegian children do not as a rule learn to read before they go to school at the age of seven.

My last picture of my great-grandfather Olsen was that he was lying in the big bed, and I was sitting beside him on the sofa. I must have fallen asleep, for the sound of his coughing startled me so much that I fell head first on to the floor. Soon after that there was a large gathering of people in the house. This must have been the funeral of the old man, for Grandpa Carlsen told me that I was to live with him in his house as my great-grandfather had gone to America and would not be back for a long time. Child-like, I accepted the situation, and looked forward to living in the house with the large ship's model.

From then on everything changed for me. Instead of spending all my days in the boat, I had to stay beside Grandma Carlsen, as Grandpa worked in the ship's yard as a rigger, but daily, just before noon, I was sent there with my grandfather's lunch. I looked forward to this because I was allowed to climb into the rigging loft where my grandfather worked, and listen with wonder as the men sang in foreign languages. These men had all been to sea in their youth, and as they worked they chanted nonsense songs in imitation of the natives of jungle countries; but I was much too young to realize then that the words were made up simultaneously with the extemporization of their melodies.

During the long fine evenings, Grandpa began to take me round to the old boat. As we set out, he tucked his old violin under his arm, and in the cabin, he treated me to fiddle music interspersed with sea shanties. Soon I learned to sing them too, and people passing by the pier stopped to listen to the sounds which came from down below, and could not help laughing when my high treble voice tried to drown the deep bass of my grandfather.

Grandpa was a popular man, and his old sea cronies used to come to the house to sit round the ship's model and hold a Saga Night. Each story capped the others regarding the storms which had to be endured and, from time to time, a finger would point to a mast or part of the rigging in illustration. I, the sole onlooker, sat spellbound. One finger which had a peculiar fascination for me was just a stump. Apparently, in the bad old days, this man's speed in climbing the rigging had not pleased the mate, who had chopped his finger off in punishment. Sometimes the room was so full of tobacco smoke that the ship was entirely obscured from view.

About a year after I went to live at my grandparent's house, my grandfather began to renovate great-grandfather Olsen's boat. "Mr Ship-owner Olsen, we go fishing together." Although I did not understand why he had given me the title of "Mr Ship-owner", I was overjoyed at the prospect of going out in the beloved boat again. Grandpa had decided that since the boat had been left to me, it would benefit us both if it were put into action. It had been a toy for old Anders Olsen, but now it would provide a living for us, and so when I was five and a half, we set out together, man and boy, to fish in earnest. My little seat was still attached to the bulkhead, but Grandpa unscrewed it, and fixed it in front of the wheel, so that I could see properly to steer the boat, while he worked with the fishing tackle and nets.

I kept asking my grandfather if I would ever have a model like the one which sat on the sitting-room table; but he misunderstood and thought that I wanted a boat to sail single-handed. "When you can swim the breadth of the river," he replied, "I'll build you a boat". The river was about 500 metres, so I practised hard at my swimming; soon I was able to satisfy my grandfather, and at the age of six, I got my very own boat in which I could sail alone. It had lugger sails, and Grandpa insisted that I must look after it myself.

During that summer, we moved into my old home by the waterfront. The house was similar to Grandpa Carlsen's, but it was more convenient for the boat, which was moored to our little private pier immediately in front of the house.

The fateful day came for me to go to school. My grandmother took me for enrolment, and I think it was then that I realized that I was in some ways different from the other boys, whose mothers proudly brought their offsprings and stood in groups chatting to each other while they waited. Grandma and I stood apart by ourselves. At the end of the morning, my grandmother returned for me, and on the way home, she bought lemonade and Danish pastries to celebrate my first day at school. This aroused the jealousy of the other children, for in the afternoon seven boys appeared on the pier beside our boat announcing that they were pirates, and were to take over the boat. Fortunately, only one could come aboard at a time. I stood on the bow awaiting the invasion, and drove my fist into the face of each intruder as he attempted to step onto the boat.

The first round gave the victory to me. Undaunted, the pirates got hold of an ancient rowing boat, and approached my boat from the other side. Picking up the *båtshake*, a long pole which had a sharp hook at the end, I warned them that I would torpedo them if they dared to come any closer. But on they came, in the old flat-sterned tub. I put out my hook, and in the effort at tugging the stern of their boat, I pulled it apart, and it immediately filled with water. Many times, I had heard my grandfather read from the Bible "Love thine enemies". Well, I could not possibly love them, but I knew that I had to save them, so I jumped on to the pier and throwing them a line,

I pulled them in. Soaking wet, and thoroughly ungrateful for my act of charity, they all ran to their homes for their mother's sympathy. Clothes changed, they returned in the evening and gave me a thorough beating up in the street.

Grandpa told me that the cause of my defeat was that I had not known the tactics of my ancestors, the Vikings, who tied their boots on very tightly before going into battle. Later I made sure that not only were my boot laces tight, but that I organized my return bout with them, one at a time, and they troubled me no more.

At that time we attended school on alternate days, having a day of freedom in between, and on those days I went fishing with my grandfather when the fjord was not frozen. Sometimes when it was the turn of my age group to go to school, I used to escape and run to a hill from which I could look out to sea and locate our boat.

My unusual background had made me tougher than most other children, and more able to resist the colds and chills which kept them off school, and I excused myself by believing that I was entitled to my freedom too. By the time I was eight years of age, I began to realize that ski-ing could be fun as well as a mode of getting about, which we take for granted in the wintertime, and the frozen river in front of the house provided wonderful skating facilities for me.

During the long dark winter evenings, Grandpa and I used to sit mending the nets which were thoroughly dried after each trip. Sometimes an acrid smell would permeate the loft and nip our noses. It was from the decayed and dried up tentacles of jellyfish which had become entangled in the nets.

After my first year at school, I began to feel the urge to travel in my own little boat, which I had named *Sigrid* after a pretty little girl of my own age. I knew every bit of the coast, and already I could navigate between the islands with ease. Oslo was to be my first target, and I invited Sigrid to come with me. Provided with a loaf of bread, some sweets, a bottle of milk, water, fishing tackle and a frying-pan—we had even coal and matches—we set sail. Passing Horten on our port side, a police launch came out and intercepted us, and we were returned to Larvik. Although Grandpa scolded us for setting out without his permission, he asked Sigrid to come out in the big boat with us for a trip. This was fun, for at sea we had a music session. Sigrid sang, Grandpa played the violin, and I the recorder. I was happy to see that she had enjoyed her outing together with us.

When we were alone again, Grandpa made me promise to tell him where we were going next time we planned a trip in the little boat. Without my knowing it at the time, he had intended to follow us.

I suggested to Sigrid one day that if we sailed to Sweden we could buy sweets cheaper than the candies which we bought in Larvik, and she thought that the idea was splendid. This time we informed Grandpa of our intended destination and set off. We were well clear of the Larvikfjord when a large steamer approached. Seeing the two children out in the open water, the captain ordered a ladder to be lowered, and still sitting in the little boat, we were hoisted aboard. I was indignant! We had to give our names and addresses, and as the ship was bound for Larvik, we were taken home by the first mate. My Grandpa told him that he had no right to interfere with our voyage as we had his permission to set out. We all returned with the mate to interview the captain, who turned out to be a kind man after all, because he gave Sigrid and I a 5 krone piece each. We were rich!

The annoyance of the interrupted voyage forgotten, we set out again; and this time, our mission accomplished, we returned with a great supply of sweets, not one of which we had touched on the journey back to Norway. Years later I discovered that Grandpa had followed us all the way, keeping out of sight between the islands.

At the age of thirteen, before leaving the local school, I applied for a place on the naval school ship. This had been my grandfather's great ambition, and he had set aside most of the money from our fishing trips for this purpose.

Prior to being accepted for this training, I had to be examined by a medical officer from the Navy as every potential cadet had to possess the top grade in physical stamina.

Then came the written examinations. The boys who intended to enter the Merchant Navy were not required to sit these, but those of us who hoped to be accepted for the Royal Navy had to pass difficult written examinations; these one could compare with the English "Common Entrance" which enables boys to enter Public schools. Accordingly, in July 1927 I was notified to present myself on board the brig *Statsråd Ericsen* to sit these examinations which were to last from Monday to Friday. After that, I returned home to await the results. Two weeks later notice arrived that I had been accepted for training. Perhaps I merely took it for granted, but my grandfather, who knew that only twenty boys from the whole of Norway were accepted each year, was very happy about it. I believe that in all over forty boys sat the papers along with me.

On the first of August my grandfather, wearing his best suit and with his white wavy hair brushed to perfection, proudly escorted me on board to attend the opening speech given to the boys and their fathers. This was a great day in my grandfather's life, as unknown to me he had geared me up for the Navy from the first day when he had become my guardian.

I went into this new stage of my life with great zeal, and within a very short time I discovered that my early introduction to sailing had placed me well ahead of my companions in seamanship. During the winter months, the training ship remained moored to the pier in Oslo, but when spring came, we moved further out the Oslofjord to Horten or Moss, while at the approach of summer we sailed as far as Denmark, and up the west coast of Norway to Trondheim.

Many times during my childhood I had heard my grandfather's old cronies refer to the lubber's hole. This could be used in emergency in bad weather by sailors who had to climb up to the mast head, but no seaman who valued his reputation would risk climbing via the lubber's hole unless given the order to do so.

At first, until we had gained courage to climb the rigging by way of the crosstrees, we had to climb via the lubber's hole. The boys who delayed taking the manly route after permission to abandon the lubber's hole had been given were jeered at by the others until they too plucked up their courage.

We were free on Saturdays and Sundays, and any boy whose home was at a distance could leave on Friday night, but had to be in class at 10 a.m. on Monday. I went home to my grandfather about once a month, but by this time I had acquired a taste for winter sports, and if I was not at the outdoor skating rink at Bislet, in Oslo, I took the tram to Frogner park to ski. If the weather was particularly fine, I climbed the slope up to the Holmenkollen hill to practise downhill and long distance ski-ing.

However much I enjoyed my life on the training ship, it was a relief to get away occasionally from the smell of tar and black oakum, and to fill my lungs with the clean fresh air of the Holmenkollen.

There were many weekends during the winter months when the weather was so bad that it was quite impossible either to go home, or to ski. Then I went to the ship's library to do extra reading. The old Saga men of my boyhood days had fired my imagination when they had told their stories about the rough weather during their sailing days, and I wanted to read more about the sailors of long ago. Stories of whale hunting in the Antarctic are familiar to most Norwegians, and I could never forget the smell from these great factory ships when they returned to discharge their cargoes in the harbours of Larvik and Sandefjord. But I particularly wanted to read about the men who had set out to find new lands, especially those who had braved the unknown waters of the Antarctic long before the whalers had arrived on the scene.

I liked to read as much as I could about the English sailor, Captain Cook, but I remember one book which I always returned to. It was a biography of a Norwegian called Captain Carsten Egebert Borchgrevink. He was born in Norway in 1864, but had emigrated to Australia in his youth. Some years later he had led an expedition to the Antarctic in a ship called the *Southern Cross*, and while some of the landing party had been ashore exploring the area round Cape Adare, the fierce Antarctic winter had suddenly set in, with the result that the ship had been trapped in the ice until the following spring.

After reading Borchgrevink's story, I concentrated most of my spare time reading on Antarctic exploration. The other books which I read were science fiction novels, particularly those of the great French writer, Jules Verne.

My two years on the *Statsråd Ericsen* passed very quickly and then I began the next stage of my career as a Naval Cadet.

I enjoyed my three years at the Royal Naval School in

Horten, for in the surrounding districts I was able to pursue my favourite winter pastime, ski-ing. My balancing act on the wheelhouse rail at the age of three had early given me an aptitude for gymnastics, and even my childish disobedience in venturing out into the cold without my scarf and mittens had me hardier than my fellow cadets. In fact I found it rather tiresome to have to wear the white scarf and brown leather gloves which were part of the Cadet uniform, and many times I was reprimanded for not wearing them. I felt the cold so little that I never troubled to wear extra clothes in the winter time, not even when flying in an open plane, although in order to protect my eyes from the icy cold wind, I wore goggles.

On the night I learnt that Rear-Admiral Byrd had selected me I sat for many hours in my lodgings in Horten, pondering over the various pictures of my childhood days which came to my mind and flashed past again to make room for another episode; somehow the kaleidoscope of my memories returned to where it had begun its rotation. I saw once more the little wall chair in the wheelhouse of my great-grandfather's boat, and I heard again the voice which I had long forgotten, saying: "Go, lad, you can do it. They need you".

I came to myself with a jolt, and looking down to the newly acquired gold stripe on my sleeve, I smiled. I had found the answer.

This stripe indicated that not only was I qualified to be a sea captain in the merchant navy, but that I had passed as a wireless operator as well as the holder of an air pilot's certificate. My early training in self-reliance and my later acquired skill in ski-ing had provided the other qualifications which were necessary to face up to the unknown hazards which lay ahead of me. And I owed everything to the love and perseverance of two old men, Great-Grandfather Olsen and Grandfather Carlsen.

CHAPTER TWO

Preparations for Adventure

Until June 1933, when the passing-out ceremony took place, I remained at the Naval base at Horten. It was quite a shock to hear my name called out as the best all-round sportsman of my year, as although I had always enjoyed athletics, it had never occurred to me that any notice had been taken of my outdoor interests. As I looked up at the Commander in astonishment, he added that my fearless qualities had been taken into account when I had been selected to join the Ellsworth Expedition to the Antarctic. My speech in reply drew laughter from my fellow sub-lieutenants as I stated that at long last I would be compelled to wear a scarf and gloves.

My immediate future settled, I naturally made some enquiries about the expedition, and in particular about the person who was to direct it.

Although the idea had been conceived by Mr Lincoln Ellsworth, he had asked Sir Hubert Wilkins to be the leader. By this time Sir Hubert had become an American citizen, but he had been born in Britain, and had received his knighthood because of his daring exploits as a flying correspondent in the Great War of 1914–1918. In 1931, he had hit the headlines of the world by being the first man to pilot a submarine under the frozen ice cap of the North Pole. His old submarine *Nautilus*, had been laid aside as no longer of any service to the United States Navy, and he was allowed to buy it for the sum of one dollar, because Naval regulations require that nothing is given away.

At that time Sir Hubert had been regarded as foolhardy to have attempted such a feat, but he had achieved it, and would have also succeeded in boring a hole through the ice cap from the waters below had the battery for operating the drill been strong enough. In disappointment, he had given up the project and had brought the old submarine to Bergen to be scrapped.

Prior to this daring attempt, Sir Hubert had spent some years in Antarctica, and with his vast knowledge of Polar conditions no one was better qualified to direct the expedition which I had been privileged to join. Sir Hubert had already bought on behalf of Mr Lincoln Ellsworth an old Norwegian seal catcher; she was a wooden ship which had been built in 1919 and registered in Aalesund under the name of *Fanefjord*. This had been a very wise choice as wooden ships can withstand the tortures inflicted by ice very much better than can modern steel ships. She had a small diesel motor, but retained her sails, fore and aft.

After she had been bought, the *Fanefjord* was placed in dry dock in Bergen to be fitted with new oak planks for ice protection, and during this time the interior of the ship was more or less renewed, while the old cargo hold was divided into sections. One of these small sections was fitted out as a ship's hospital, although few people could have recognized it as such, for it contained only a table and some lockers for holding instruments and medicines.

When I joined the ship in June, she was no longer called the *Fanefjord* but the *Wyatt Earp*, after a famous hunter who was a friend of Mr Lincoln Ellsworth. Across its sides, were painted in bold letters ELLSWORTH EXPEDITION. It was exciting to join such a ship although she was so tiny, only 400 tons d.w.

The press and other people kept asking permission to come aboard. Among those who were allowed to look over the ship was my father, Captain Hartvig Olsen, as his ship, a passenger cargo vessel of the Fred Olsen Line, was lying at anchor nearby. But visitors had to be forbidden when the loading of provisions began.

Crate after crate was delivered to the ship to be stowed away immediately. We had to have double the amount of rations required for our stay in the Antarctic, in case we were beset by ice and could not get away. The boxes of clothing contained not only those required for the polar regions, but garments for the tropics as well, since we had to cross the equator on our way to the far South.

It was thrilling to take delivery of the plane. The *Polar Star* was much too large to be carried all the way on the deck of such a little ship, and it had to be completely dismantled and packed in its own compartment in the hold of the ship. After it was safely stowed away, we took on oil for the engines and barrels of petrol for the plane. Lastly came a large supply of fresh water for drinking.

There were seventeen of us in all, from Mr Ellsworth to the cabin boy. On board every one had to play a double role, in order to comply with safety regulations. The ship was too tiny to permit more crew members, and for that reason the chief air pilot had to act as first mate at sea, while I had to be the second mate. Even the ship's doctor, an American, had to sign on for the voyage as an ordinary seaman and, as such, he had to take his spells of duty at the wheel, and even had to clean out the fo'c'sle head.

The ship was then ready for sea, very well loaded and completely secured; our two lifeboats were well stocked with emergency provisions. The Board of Trade inspectors checked every detail, and we sailed with their Certificate of Seaworthiness for our Antarctic expedition.

My cabin was a very tiny one, just large enough to hold a bunk, a washstand, and a three-tier bookcase. There was floor space sufficient only for me to stand, but I had it to myself; little did I know then that it was to be my home for three long years.

CHAPTER THREE

To Capetown

The quay at Bergen had been packed to capacity all morning that sunny day in early August 1933 to see the little ship *Wyatt Earp* depart for her fantastic voyage. There was tense excitement by noon, when, flag bedecked, she finally slipped from her moorings, amid a storm of cheers from the shore, and the hooting of sirens from the big ships which were in dock and at anchorage.

We did not set out alone, as hundreds of small craft, yachts, motorboats, and fishing boats escorted us to the inner lighthouse. From every direction came shouts of "Good Luck" and "Bon Voyage", as well as the general noise of the hooters and whistles from the small boats.

The crew of the *Wyatt Earp* were all on deck acknowledging the good wishes. Above us, hanging from the foremast to the aftermast, were the international code signal flags, while fluttering at the top of the foremast itself was the flag of the United States of America, as we were an American Expedition. Hoisted immediately below it was the British Red Ensign, because we were heading for territory which was first explored and claimed by the British. Below these two great flags hung about twenty-five ensigns of world famous explorer's clubs. Alone at the stern of the ship hung the national flag of Norway, because the ship was registered at Aalesund, and in honour of the late Roald Amundsen who had been a great friend of Mr Lincoln Ellsworth and who had been the first to reach the South Pole.

When we reached the inner lighthouse, we took leave of our escorting flotilla by dipping the Norwegian flag and blowing three long hoots on the ship's siren in salute and farewell.

At this point we took the inner approaches instead of heading straight for the North Sea. That means that we sailed southwards between the islands, passing Stord Island on the inner side nearby to Leirvik. Out past the smaller islands, we approached Haugesund, and kept close to the island Karmöy, passing first Kopervik, then on to the southern part at Skudeneshavn; this is the pilot station for inshore routes, but our ship was so small and the route so well known to us, we did not require a pilot. From there we headed straight for the North Sea, north of Stavanger, with a course heading for the Goodwin lightship in the English Channel.

When we came out into the open sea there was a heavy north-westerly swell, although the westerly wind was very light, but before dusk fell we observed big dark clouds around the horizon. This spelt bad weather ahead. Already the swell was growing higher, and the barometer began to fall. But nothing untoward happened during the night. In early morning we sailed into heavy rain, and the wind increased and veered to the north-west. The ship began to roll heavily, because the swell hit us on the starboard side. To steady the ship and to increase the speed, we hoisted the sails, fore and aft. Soon the ship was steadied, and it also increased our speed from 5 knots to 8 knots.

That gale, which lasted two full days, proved to us that our little ship was indeed seaworthy, and we continued our journey in full confidence that she would be able to withstand any weather.

In ideal conditions we continued our voyage, then the weather became so hot that by the time we were passing to the east side off Fuerteventura Island, we had to change into tropical clothing. From Cape Verde we hugged the coast to Freetown in Sierra Leone, then set course for St Helena Island in the South Atlantic Ocean. The weather was so unbearably hot that we were forced to sleep out on deck, under tarpaulins, to shelter from the tropical rain storms.

As we sailed nearer to the equator, our minds turned to fancy dress costumes in preparation for Crossing the Line. The ceremony of King Neptune coming aboard is of very ancient origin, but it is carried out to this day. Every person who has not crossed the equator before has to be admitted into

23

Neptune's Kingdom, and as only few of us had already earned our Certificate of Initiation we had to conduct the ceremony of initiating the others. Consequently the steward was chosen to be King Neptune and was arrayed in a robe of combed out manila ropes in imitation of seaweed. He looked very resplendent in his gold crown, constructed from a tin which had once held butter. The messboy was similarly dressed up as the Queen. One of the able seamen assumed the guise of a doctor and carried a bag conspicuously labelled MEDICUS. His duty was to examine the candidates for acceptance into "Neptune's Kingdom". Of course it was arranged that every candidate had to suffer from some kind of sickness, for which the doctor was to prescribe a medicine, beforehand we had concocted various pills and liquids, such as the real ship's doctor would not have dared to prescribe; bottles were filled with a mixture of vinegar and soda water and coloured with whatever the steward could supply; pills were made of flour, a good supply of pepper and salt, plus whatever bitter flavouring we could find. We certainly made sure that they were exceedingly unpalatable.

Another part of the ritual is the soaping and shaving, so the second engineer was elected to be the barber, and had for his "Tool of Trade" a gigantic wooden open razor. The other able seaman baptized the initiates. It was decided that I should be dressed as the chief police inspector to act as Neptune's guard and to hand out the certificates.

Before the ceremony began the candidates were assembled aft, while King Neptune and his retinue were hidden behind canvas on the forepart of the ship; then as we crossed the equator, the ship's bell was struck, the whistle blew, and the engines stopped. The Captain stood midships to welcome Neptune's party, then came the candidates who had at once to submit to medical examination and the follow up cure. After a visit to the barber, they were dipped several times in a barrel of water. Thoroughly soaked, they received their certificates, and were accepted as worthy inhabitants of "Neptune's Kingdom".

Ceremony over, the command "Full speed ahead" was given to the engine room; the engine was restarted and the sails set for a light easterly breeze. Yet the celebrations were continued into the evening when everyone was treated to special delicacies, and we ended the day with a sing-song on deck.

We were more than half way to Capetown, so we had to begin in earnest to check all our polar clothing and equipment. Our ship had to be repainted and treated with a preparation made from tar for our sojourn in the Antarctic waters.

Approaching St Helena we sighted first its highest point, High Hill (2,823 ft), a mountain which must have been a familiar sight to Napoleon Bonaparte during the last few years of his life when he was imprisoned on the island.

Soon an albatross came to greet us. This great bird belongs only to the southern hemisphere, and has never been known to cross north of the equator.

Daily from then onwards, early morning until dusk, sometimes as many as ten of them came hovering round the ship to eat the remains of our meals which were thrown overboard. The albatross never alights on a ship, and goes to the water only when food is thrown out. No sailor can resist watching an albatross in flight. It has a pure white body and its grey wings can reach a span of nearly 6 feet. Only a slight movement of its wings is seen, so this bird gives the impression that it is always gliding.

Thus far we had been living on tinned food and salted meat, but we had reached the native waters of the bonito: it is similar to a mackerel, but very much more delicious, so we ate it every day. Our method of catching it was somewhat unorthodox; we placed a hook on a long line covered with highly coloured bits of cloth, such as torn flags, and these were dipped into gravy or the remains of the soup pot. The bait then both looked and smelt attractive to the fish.

"Blue Thursday" must not be forgotten when giving an account of our menus. We had learned to dread our Thursday lunch as the main dish consisted of pemmican, so that we would become accustomed to its taste before we reached the Antarctic. It is a preparation first used by the North American Indians, and consists of the lean parts of buffalo, which are first dried and reduced to powder, then mixed in boiling fat; the mixture was finally dried in the form of cakes. Many years before our expedition British Arctic expeditions had discovered its value as emergency rations, and later it became a compulsory item on the provision list for all polar expeditions. We had a factory prepared version which was sealed in air-tight tins, but we fervently hoped that no emergency would compel us to live on it.

After St Helena we set our course for Walvis Bay, where a school of whales came very close to the ship. These were the sperm whales or cachalot; they are gigantic mammals, some of them reaching 60 feet in length, of which one-third is the head. They are hunted not only for their oil but also for their teeth, which are in the lower jaw and these make valuable ivory. Ambergris, which is a secretion from the sperm whales, found floating on the water, is used as a basis for many expensive perfumes. These monsters exist mainly on a diet of cuttlefish, and to catch them they must dive to the bottom of the ocean.

Soon after we had encountered the whales we began to meet whale-catching ships; they were based at Walvis Bay, where there was also a large whale oil factory belonging to a British firm. In all, we passed about five whaling ships and we exchanged salutes with each other by dipping our flags.

From then on we met ships day and night until we came to Capetown. A few days before we sighted Table Mountain we were greeted by the cape pigeons, which filled the air and made a feather carpet on the sea; they escorted us all the way to land.

On the 24th September we sailed into Capetown Harbour and moored the ship to one of the piers inside the large breakwater.

CHAPTER FOUR

Through the Roaring Forties

We were delighted to hear the news that there was another Norwegian ship in the harbour, and were glad to accept the offer to go on board and have hot fresh water baths.

This was an absolute luxury to us, as, on our trip from Bergen, our daily ration of fresh water for washing purposes had been one bucketful each of cold water, and we had mainly to wash ourselves in salt water, using a special soap for the purpose. We all felt most refreshed and relaxed when we returned to our little ship, and we lazed about for the remainder of the day.

The following morning we began in earnest our preparations for entering the frozen waters of the Antarctic. The *Polar Star* aircraft had to be taken on deck for cleaning, as it had been greased with a special preparation to prevent corrosion during the voyage from Bergen. Over the grease, the body of the plane had been wrapped in sheets of oiled paper, which we had to remove. We covered the foredeck hatch with new tarpaulin, on top of which we built a frame to support and secure the plane; it took several days to complete this operation, as we had to use meticulous care at every stage.

The compartment of the hold which had previously housed the *Polar Star*, had next to be cleaned before using it to lay out the equipment and polar clothing; these had previously been stowed in out-of-reach lockers, but every item had to be accessible and ready for use.

Personal equipment consisted of two pairs of snow shoes and two pairs of skis for each man. These were painted bright orange in colour so that they could be seen from a distance. On the underside at the back of the skis were fixed 8-inch long strips of seal-skin to prevent sliding backwards when we were climbing hills or pulling sledges. (We took no dogs with us.)

1. 1933–34 Season

28

The special boots which we had to wear while ski-ing were made of leather; they were sewn throughout with waxed cord and lined with thick sheep-skin. To prevent frost-bite, we were provided with boots two sizes larger than our normal footwear.

The lifeboats had to be restocked with fresh drinking water, and the provisions rechecked. Emergency clothing was stacked in waterproof air-tight tanks, and to these items were added fishing tackle, cooking utensils and a rifle.

While the ship was being reloaded with drums of lubricating oil and engine fuel (we carried 160 drums in all on deck), the work of stacking was disturbed by spectators, who tried to board the ship, so we moved the *Wyatt Earp* from the pier altogether and dropped anchor in a position with the stern to the breakwater, where we could continue our work without interruption.

After the oil drums had been secured, we took on another little plane for scouting purposes. It was so small that it was placed, complete, aft on the boat-deck.

Last to be brought on board was a supply of meat, which we hung up on the foremast rigging. The reason for the strange position of our larder was that the wind would dry the meat. Of course, the flags had been removed long before this, and only one remained at the top of the mast; this was the British Red Ensign, because we were on our way to territory in the Antarctic which had been first sighted and claimed by the British.

We slipped away from Capetown early on the morning of 9th October 1933, and at last we were able to set our course for the Antarctic.

About five days after we had left the shelter of Capetown Harbour, we felt instinctively that we were drawing near to the Roaring Forties. That is, we were approaching the half-way area of the southern hemisphere where the cold air from the south meets the hot air from the north. This is the region of the anti-trade winds, and although they blow generally from a steady direction, usually north-west, the force is so unpredictable that they can vary in minutes from a gentle breeze to a full storm.

For this reason, the mate on duty had to check the barometer every half-hour or so; whenever it began to fall in this part of the world we had to be prepared for bad weather.

Once into the Forties the temperature fell so much that we were compelled to return to our warmer clothing. We had our first fog of our journey together with a westerly wind which caused the waves to hurtle against the ship's side, sending up a spray which drenched the decks. We had already learned the value of our sails during the gale in the North Sea, and here again the sails came to our aid by giving us a list to port, thus lessening the roll of the ship.

One person who thoroughly disliked the heel of the ship was the steward, as the contents of the pots and pans tended to spill, but to avoid a big mess, he placed wooden wedges below the left legs of the stove, and kept handy a large collection of different sized wedges. Thus we began to gauge the strength of the wind by the thickness of the wedges which the steward had selected to balance the pots; from then on, he was nicknamed the Weather Man.

We had to keep a regular look-out for drifting ice, although at that stage we had not seen any. But every day the temperature fell. We had to pay attention to the water as well to the air, and for this purpose there was a mechanism on board which registered the temperature of the sea water; it was worked by a pump from the engine room, and connected by a pipe to a gauge in the wheel-house. A sudden drop indicated the presence of ice.

A full gale in latitude 48° S. signified that at last we were in the heart of the Roaring Forties. Instead of abating, the gale increased to a full storm, and we had to heave-to. That means that we were forced to alter course, so that the waves hit the starboard bow, and instead of sailing straight ahead, we were riding the waves at an angle of 45°. However, we were compelled by the force of the wind to take down our mainsail as we were heeling too much, but we left the foresail and the mizzen. We tried to persevere with these, but had to give in and take down the foresail as well. In doing so, we regained full control of the ship, although she was still pitching and rolling heavily. In spite of the mountainous seas, only the crest of an occasional wave broke over the ship.

We made very little headway at this stage, and the turbulence of the water prevented the log-line from functioning, as all it could do was to dip up and down. To make matters worse, the visibility was very poor because of the sea spray and haze. At most, we could see only about 50 yards distance. Some days went by when we could make no observations, and all we could do was to guess our position by dead reckoning.

Our course was set to a point east of the southern islands of the Sandwich Group, so that should the ship be damaged or the engine threaten to fail, we could seek some shelter for repairs before we entered the dangerous waters of the Weddell Sea.

Before I continue the story of our little ship, which is probably one of the smallest vessels ever to have braved the violent storms in the dangerous waters which surround the vast Southern Continent, I will summarize what I had read about the Antarctic during the months prior to our departure, and in moments of free time on board.

Today the term Great Ice Barrier is very familiar to everyone, but I expect that there are many who accept it without understanding what this awesome phenomenon is. Surrounding the coast of the continent and islands are colossal rocks, mountains, and even volcanoes. At the approach of winter, over millions of years, freezing water thrown up against these rocks has caused a vast accumulation of ice to project from them; above the surface of the sea it rises to over 200 feet, while the frozen projection below the surface reaches a depth of nearly 1,500 feet. This is the Great Ice Barrier.

During the months of the Antarctic spring and summer, the ice calves. That is, it breaks from the land, and divides into icebergs. On separation from the parent ice, the berg sinks until its submerged portion is nine times that visible above the water, yet some of these icebergs are so colossal that they are frequently mistaken for islands. Some have actually been charted and claimed for their countries by early explorers who were unable to find them on their return another year.

Even a modern ship might take several days to sail round one of the largest bergs.

For any exploration of the Antarctic one has to calculate carefully when to set out so as to make the approach during the Antarctic summer. One could say that midsummer in Antarctica falls on Christmas Day, so that the best months are from November to the middle of February. Then the fierce winter storms begin, and perpetual darkness falls.

But no matter the time of year, an explorer has to understand what each element of the weather produces. For instance, the northerly winds produce snow and fog, while the southerly winds blowing from the Pole produce the lowest temperatures when the waters freeze and throw up against the barrier. When this happens, the pack ice solidifies to one mass, and a ship can be encased in it for a whole winter until the approach of summer and the ice breaks again.

The knowledge of this vast Southern Continent, its fearsome approaches, its hazards, and its awesome beauty, is due to the various explorers over a period of two centuries. Each one contributed a small but invaluable piece of evidence; each made his own charts, although some of the early latitude and longitude observations are today regarded as doubtful, as the old instrument for taking observations, the octant, differs from the modern sextant.

CHAPTER FIVE

Early Antarctic Explorers

It is not known who first sailed to the Antarctic, as there have been various unproven claims as far back as 200 years before the English mariner James Cook, the son of a Yorkshire farm labourer, made his first voyage to the Southern Seas during the three years period from 1772 to 1775. The expedition which Cook commanded consisted of two ships, the *Resolution* and the *Adventure*.

They crossed the Antarctic circle for the first time in history on 17th January 1773, and the purpose of the whole expedition was to determine the extent of the Southern Continent about which there had been many reports by sailors who had deviated from their routes.

During this first attempt they did not reach land, but skirted the ice in high latitude before heading for New Zealand the following October. In the Southern Seas the *Adventure* somehow become separated from Cook's *Resolution*, and returned to England. Cook sailed on to New Zealand without her and from there he sailed again towards the South Polar regions; in January 1774, he encountered the great ice mass once more, this time in latitude 71° 10' S. and longitude 106° 54' W. From here he explored some of the many islands in the Southern Pacific, then set sail in the direction of Cape Horn. It was on this journey that he sighted South Georgia and the Sandwich Lands.

The Navy then promoted Cook to the rank of captain, and in the following year, he was placed in charge of a second expedition to the Pacific. Once again, he commanded the *Resolution* while the second ship sent on this expedition was the *Discovery* with Captain Clerke in charge. The two ships set off by different routes, but joined company at Capetown; on the way to the

South Pacific they visited the islands which Captain Cook had sighted previously, and gave them their names South Georgia and the Sandwich Group. South Georgia is a fairly large island, while the Sandwich Group contains about nine tiny islands grouped almost in a semi-circle.

It was not until over forty years later, in 1819, that another British explorer named William Smith succeeded in reaching islands which lie close to the great central land mass. He named them the South Shetland Islands.

Other countries were eager to be represented in the great quest for the southernmost land. Thus in 1819 Captain Bellinghausen, a Russian, set out on an expedition which was to last two years. He first visited South Georgia and the Sandwich Group, which had been discovered by Captain Cook, and sailed south to discover an island in 68° 50′ S. and 92° 19′ W. He named this island Peter First Island, but as he did not land on it, he could not claim it for his country. It now belongs to Norway, as in 1929 a party from the *Norvegia* expedition landed on it and hoisted the Norwegian flag. Sailing northeasterly from this point Bellinghausen discovered what he believed to be a piece of coast line of the continent which he named Alexander First Land. This is in 69° 00′ S. and 72° 00′ W., but later proved to be an island.

Soon a series of explorers came on the scene. In 1822, James Weddell concentrated his investigations in a large bay in the South Atlantic Ocean, off the north-east coast of the mainland of Antarctica; this stretch of water has been named after him the Weddell Sea. Ten years later, farther south and east in the Indian Ocean, the English sailor, John Biscoe, sighted land in 67° 20′ S. and 49° 47′ E. He named it Enderby Land after his employer. He discovered also the most northerly part of the Antarctic Continent which was later named Graham Land. This part is connected by a vast submarine shelf with Cape Horn at the most southerly toe of South America.

On the Pacific side of the continent is an inlet called Biscoe Bay, which Captain Scott entered on his first expedition years later.

During the years 1830 to 1840 several islands round the coast were sighted and named. In many cases, the thrill of discovery was followed by disillusionment, for what appeared at the time to be great stretches of land were later proved to be tiny islands; this was due to the difficulty of estimating the area of land, owing to the extent of the ice shelf which surrounded it.

In 1840, two ships left Hobart in Tasmania to explore the South Polar Seas. They were the *Terror* and *Erebus* under the command of Captain Sir James Clark Ross, a Scotsman born in Wigtownshire. He was accompanied by Sir Joseph Hooker, and much more knowledge was gained on this expedition than on any which had gone before. They made a landing on the ice shelf near Biscoe Bay, and were able to trace the coast line for about 570 miles. They named several mountains and volcanoes, two of them after their ships; Mount Erebus is over 12,000 feet, while Mount Terror, now extinct, is over 10,000 feet. Another important find on this expedition, was the location of the South Magnetic Pole, in 75° 05′ S., and 154° 08′ E. Subsequent explorations have established that mounts Terror and Erebus are not on the mainland, but are in fact on an island.

A Belgian expedition set out in 1898, under the command of Captain de Gerlache. It had to spend a complete winter in the Antarctic, because their ship, the *Belgica*, was beset by ice in 71° 31′ S. and 85° 16′ W. This was in the same year that Captain Borchgrevink had wintered off Cape Adare.

From then onwards, several important large-scale expeditions were carried out. In 1901 a wooden ship was built in Dundee, Scotland, for the British National Antarctic Exploration and named the *Discovery*. She was placed under the command of Captain R. F. Scott, R.N. In late 1902, the expedition entered the ice pack, near the place where Sir James Clark Ross first landed. They followed the Ross Barrier for a considerable distance to the east, finding that in 165° 00′ W., it trends to the north. In this region they found heavily glaciated land with occasional bare peaks rising from the barrier. They named this King Edward VII Land. On 1st January 1903, accompanied by Lieut. Shackleton, Captain Scott sledged to 82° 17′ S. and placed the British flag. This was the highest southern latitude yet attained.

The Scottish National Antarctic Expedition using the ship *Scotia* explored the Weddell Sea in 1902. After wintering in the South Orkney Islands, she returned to the Weddell Sea the following year and carried out dredging operations in an area known as Ross Deep. Sir James Clark Ross had sounded this patch of water years before, and had recorded his observation as no bottom at 4,000 fathoms. The Scotia crew proved that it was actually 2,600 fathoms deep.

One of the most amazing stories of Antarctic survival was that of the Swedish expedition which left Europe in 1901 in the ship *Antarctica*. Their ship was wrecked by the ice, but the whole party survived, salvaged what they could of the wreckage, and built a hut from it. In this they managed to survive for three years when they were rescued.

In 1911, the Norwegian explorer Roald Amundsen sailed for the Antarctic in the ship *Fram* with Fritjof Nansen as its captain. They took skis as part of their equipment, and dogs to pull the sledges with the provisions and other necessary equipment. On 14th December of that year, they reached the South Pole, at a height which was thought to have been 8,500 feet above sea level although later it was proved that the South Pole peak is 10,260 feet high. They claimed for Norway a radius of 110 miles round it.

This was the great tragedy for Captain Scott and his party. The whole world expected that he would have been the first man to reach the South Pole, but when they reached the summit on 18th January 1912, they found to their dismay that the Norwegian flag was already there. The general opinion is that had Captain Scott used dogs instead of ponies to carry tents and food he would have won the race to the Pole. The heavier animals, the ponies, could not tackle the tasks which were more natural to a team of huskies.

The great Captain Scott died of cold and frost-bite, and as death approached he continued to write his diary, which has been a great source of inspiration to others, as well as a wealth of information about the Antarctic.

In the 1920s the United States of America planned an expedition on a scale which had never before been attempted. It was placed under the command of Rear-Admiral Richard Evelyn Byrd, U.S.N. (my unknown passenger at Horten). This expedition, which required many years of preparation, consisted of two ships large enough to carry several planes between them as the main objective of the expedition was to penetrate the interior of the continent.

Once arrived, the *Ruppert* was to act as the depotship, while the *Bear of Oakland* was to stand by as a safeguard to the men. The expedition finally set out in 1929; they landed on the Ross Sea Barrier, not far from the region where Captain Scott had left his ship on the 1903 expedition. The Americans called this place the Bay of Whales.

Six members of the team set up a base camp in 78° 40' S. and 160° 00' W. This was 2½ hours ski-ing distance from the depot ship and they called it Little America; it was the first official base in the history of Antarctic study. Here they were able to assemble instruments to measure the velocity of the wind and the direction of air currents.

Now we have brought the story to the time when the little ship *Wyatt Earp* entered the Antarctic waters for the first time.

CHAPTER SIX

Problems of the Antarctic

On the morning of 21st October, after four days of battling with the storm, the weather cleared suddenly, enabling us to take several observations from the sun. These showed our position to be 48° 20' S. and 05° 36' W.

In the afternoon, we sailed into small patches of drifting pack ice, and from then onwards we were constantly on the alert for larger patches or even icebergs. In anticipating those hazards we were not afraid as even the greatest dangers can be turned to advantage. We decided therefore that as soon as we spotted an iceberg we should approach it from the leeward side, and thereby use it as a sheltering breakwater.

When evening came, the south horizon appeared to be one solid mass of white. We were approaching the ice pack, and we had no alternative but to enter it. So we manœuvred about until we could find an opening through which we could begin to plough our way in.

The noise of the ice against the sides of the ship, as we crunched through it, was exactly like the sound of a stone crushing machine in a granite quarry.

However, we managed to force our way into the pack ice to a distance of about two miles, where there was only a slight undulating movement on the ice. Here we were able to place our bow to head the swell, and only then was it possible for us to relax and rest. We stopped the engine and secured the rudder, so that the only noises we heard were the grating and rasping of the ice as it rose and fell, and the noise of the storm as it howled and whistled through the rigging.

At 11 p.m., we were summoned to the mess room to partake of the *Smörgosbord* which the steward had prepared. It was an unexpected treat to see such a traditional Norwegian festive table so far from home and under such conditions. There in front of us was the usual selection of beefburgers with onions, cold ham, smoked salmon, cold boiled trout, shrimps in mayonnaise, and tit-bits of herring and anchovies cured in wine and spices. There were also several of our Norwegian cheeses, including *Geitost* which is made from goat's milk. Of course this feast would not have been possible but for the invention of the food canning processes. I must not omit to say that there was an ample helping of tinned fruit and cream for each to round off the meal.

Everyone has heard Norway described as the Land of the Midnight Sun. This refers to the most northerly part of the country from Bodö to the North Cape, where, at midsummer, the sun does not set and there are 24 hours of daylight. But Norway is a very long country, and in the town of Larvik, which is south of Oslo, daylight conditions are a little different. There at midsummer the sun does set, but since it rises again in a few hours there is no real darkness in June, only twilight. Few people realize that this is also the case in the northern part of Scotland. From the Moray Firth and northwards, darkness in summer only means dusk.

At corresponding latitudes of the southern hemisphere, the same conditions prevail, except that midsummer falls in December instead of in June. Therefore, as we enjoyed our *Smörgosbord* that night, we were in no peril from darkness, as we were in the spring of the southern hemisphere when the sun is south of the equator.

Although the pack ice was no higher than from 2 to 5 feet, it gave us the shelter which we required, making it possible to spend the next day there, searching for any likely damage to the ship or to the contents of the holds. Contrary to what we expected, nothing was wrong, our little ship had proved once again how sturdy she was. While in the shelter of the ice, we had drifted with it and we therefore had to take observations to find out how far we had drifted. Our findings gave us the necessary information regarding the strength and direction of the sea current, and revealed that we were drifting eastward.

We remained in the pack ice for two days, and after breakfast on 23rd October we made preparations to push our way southwards. The zone of the pack ice must have been greater area than we had at first anticipated, because the sky of the south horizon was white; this is caused by reflection from ice, as otherwise the sky would have been dark blue. Our situation necessitated the crow's nest on top of the foremast being manned, so the sailors took hourly spells on duty to search for a region where we could force a lane through the pack ice. A patch of open water would have given us the chance to gain momentum when we came to it.

The full storm had reduced to gale force from a westerly direction, so we hoisted all sails to give us more power to thrust our way ahead. One very real danger was the possibility of the propeller being damaged by the big ice lumps. (A piece of ice 5 feet high, indicates 45 feet below the surface.) While passing through an ice-field, a ship can never keep on a straight course, and we had to zigzag our way, alternating between south-east, and south-west.

Early the following morning, after nearly 24 hours of struggling through the ice, the look-out man shouted "Dark blue sky ahead". This information came as a great relief to all, for it meant that we were heading for open water again.

Because of the westerly gale, we altered course slightly to the south-east, so that we took the sea on our starboard quarter, and the speed increased to 9 knots. As the barometer had already begun to rise, we decided to keep to that course until the weather cleared and conditions were entirely favourable to head for the Weddell Sea.

At 4 p.m. on 27th October, our position was 56° 40′ S., 02° 15′ E. The skies cleared and the sun shone, but our course had been altered so much that we were no longer sailing in the direction of the Sandwich Group Islands. Accordingly we reset our course for a point 70° 00′ S. and 18° 00′ W., in the eastern approach to the Weddell Sea.

Although we had reached open water, we were drawing very close to the maximum limit zone of pack ice surrounding the Antarctic Continent. At any time we could encounter drifting icebergs, but we were able to continue our course from 56° 40′ S. and 02° 15′ E. for 180 miles before we reached the solid pack ice at 60° 00′ S. and 04° 15′ W.

On entering the pack ice we used the methods which our

previous experience in the ice-field had taught us. This time it was much more compact than the drifting patches of ice had been, and we had no alternative but to force our way by ploughing the ship through. The ice, however, was our friend as well as our foe, as it prevented a heavy swell on the sea.

Reflection from ice can impair the eyesight, therefore we had to wear dark glasses, as well as the black eye shields which projected from our caps. As I have already mentioned, our decks were tar painted, and the dark colour of the ship gave us relief from the glare of the ice which surrounded us.

There were many seals lying on the ice floes, but curiously they paid no attention to us unless by chance the ship hit the submerged part of the ice on which they were lying; then they dived into the water between the ice lumps to reappear further away, when they turned to inspect the monster which had disturbed their peace. We killed one of them occasionally when we needed fresh meat; but seal meat is so strong, that it must be soaked in vinegar for 24 hours before use to remove the blubber. Even then, it was only mixed with flour and seasonings to make meat balls, as we did not dare to eat it as solid meat. Nevertheless, we found our seal-meat balls very delicious. This species of seal is known as the Leopard because of its black-spotted yellow coat, but none of the Antarctic seals are hunted for their fur, as their hairs are too loose.

We had a very long, hard struggle to reach the point of entry to the Weddell Sea, because the nearer we came to it, the more we realized that we were facing, not pack ice only, but large drifting icebergs; so it was not until 21st November that we reached 70° 00′ S. and 18° 00′ W.

At last we were approaching the Great Ice Barrier. From the books I had read when I was on the *Statsråd Ericsen*, I had pictured the scene to be a vast whiteness in which the icebergs would predominate, but all would be silent, still, and lifeless. How very different it was when I reached the Weddell Sea. It was alive! As the ship wended its way precariously through the heaving ice-sludge, and between the patches of swirling pack ice, and tortuously twisting icebergs, I realized that these frozen waters were the home of countless of living creatures.

The first to greet us were the nodding and bowing penguins which looked exactly like a team of head waiters, each anxious to pilot us to his own particular table. Lying on ice floes were hundreds of seals sunning themselves, while patches of bright red plankton drew our attention to the blue and fin-back whales which tumbled about in between the patches of ice, while they made their meal of the myriads of minute shrimp-like creatures that drifted helplessly in their millions.

On our port side was the Great Ice Barrier, rising from 60 feet to over 200 feet high. The noice caused by the mighty under-water currents heaving the great icebergs against the ice shelf was even louder than the crashing thunderstorms which we had experienced near the equator.

The strange and eerie grandeur around us had such a hypnotic effect on us all that we seemed to be unable to leave the deck rail and retire to rest.

It was quite out of the question for us to attempt to moor the ship, as a heaving iceberg would have crushed the little *Wyatt Earp* to matchwood; so we followed the barrier further into the Weddell Sea. On 25th November we approached a bay where, along with five others, I managed to make a landing. It is called Vahsel Bay, and is approximately 76° 25′ S., and 31° 00′ W.

We remained there for only a few hours, and when we returned to the ship the current had begun to increase so much, that we had to head at once for Palmer Land, which is south of Graham Land. We were so enthused at the thought of the adventures which lay ahead that we almost forgot about the dangers which surrounded us as we zigzagged our way between the colossal icebergs. Nevertheless, we were in great peril, for had either the engine failed or the rudder been damaged, our total destruction would have been inevitable.

In 73° 16′ S. and 55° 30′ W. we were relieved to find that the ice-free patches of water had widened, and that the current had decreased considerably. A strong westerly wind had caused the ice pack to drift away from the barrier, and we were able to take advantage of its shelter without the fear of being crushed by the icebergs which previously had been crashing up against the shelf.

We were steering in a channel of ice-free water in a true northerly direction. When we reached 70° 05′ S. and 59° 30′ W., we noticed that we were approaching a small island with a lagoon which was completely free of drifting ice and where it would be easy to make a landing.

We entered the lagoon at dead slow speed, and to make sure that we had sufficient depth of water below the keel, we threw out our sounding line; this means that a member of the crew stood at the bow and threw a line ahead of the ship into the water; it was 20 fathoms long and knotted at each fathom with a coloured cord. As its leaded end never touched the bottom, we were quite safe, but the process was kept up continuously until we reached the barrier. Then a ladder was put up from the ship so that the crew members could go ahead to be ready to receive the ice anchors when they were swung ashore by the ship's derricks. Each anchor was hoisted over together with a sledge. First the sledge was unhooked, then the anchor placed on top of it and dragged to a suitable place for mooring. The remainder of the operation was done from the ship.

We had hoped that from there either Bernt Balchen or myself could take off in the scouting plane to find a potential runway for the *Polar Star*, because it was 29th November and well into the Antarctic summer; but again we had to admit defeat because of the weather, and all we could do was to return to the ship and check the engine again. Thereafter we took it in turns to have a good night's sleep as it was essential that at least one person should be on the look out for ice danger.

Next day, we left the lagoon with our course set for Jason Island, in 66° 00′ S. and 63° 40′ W., sailing still in the direction of true north. The further north we sailed, the more the weather deteriorated, with cloudy skies and snow blizzards; but as the wind was still from the west, we were able to benefit from the shelter provided by the ice barrier.

We saw Jason Island from the distance only as we passed, but the ice conditions made it impossible for us to approach it. There was nothing we could do but to sail as close as possible to Palmer Land, and Graham Land, then head for a strip of water known as Hell's Gate, through which we hoped to reach Deception Island.

Before reaching this small island, we passed James Ross Island, Snow Hill Island, Dundee Island, and Joinsville Island, which are grouped near the north-east tip of Graham Land.

Hell's Gate is well-named as it is probably the most danger-ous strip of water in the world. Here the westerly currents meet those from the east, resulting in large drifting icebergs coming from opposite directions to crash against each other; they split, sending off large lumps of ice, which in turn collect to form patches of pack ice.

It was still blowing from the west when we entered Hell's Gate, and as we were steering into the gale the ship began to pitch heavily; but in spite of hazards we continued on our way, and came through the dangerous water unscarred.

CHAPTER SEVEN

Deception Island

On 5th December we approached Deception Island. This is one of the South Shetland group which was discovered and named by William Smith in 1819, and is therefore British territory. For many years this island had been used by a Norwegian whaling company, but the base had closed down in the mid-1920s. As we approached we first sighted a lighthouse at the entrance of the harbour, while on our starboard side stood a rock, named the Sewing Machine because of its likeness to one when seen from a distance. As we passed the rock, we faced a narrow channel leading to the ice-covered harbour in front of the whaling station. Although we were very close to the pier it took us a long time before we could finally moor the ship because of the drifting ice.

Nature had formed this harbour in an extinct volcano; the opening was very narrow and had a depth of only 26 fathoms. Once into the harbour, which was completely round, the water was so deep that although we used a sounding line of 200 fathoms, it was not long enough to measure the depth.

Encircling the harbour were high mountains of volcanic rock, but the area on which the whaling station had been built was flat. Presumably it had once been a shelf within the crater walls, as on the beach in front of the buildings we found places where the sand was warm, while further inshore the sand was so hot that large patches were completely free of ice and snow.

At one time this island had been the scene of a thriving industry, but for the previous eight years it had been derelict. Only the abandoned buildings and equipment were left to tell the story of the activities of bygone days.

Although all the buildings had belonged to one company, Nils Bugge & Co, of Tönsberg, at least a dozen factory ships belonging to other Norwegian whale oil companies would have been lying in the shelter of the harbour. Plying to and from the deep waters outside would have been many small whale catching ships; some of which would have supplied the factory ships, while the others would have belonged to the resident company and would have delivered their catches to the factory on the island.

In all, the population on and around Deception Island must have been more than 2,500 men. Of these, about 650 men would have been employed on the mainland, and the others on the whale oil factory ships and on the many small ships harpooning the whales.

Leading from the beach was a large slipway, over which the bodies of the whales would have been dragged and flenched, before being delivered to the factory. Some of the monsters which had been harpooned and dragged to shore must have weighed about 100 tons.

The pier beside which our little ship was moored had been constructed for the whale catching ships and was quite small, only about 150 feet long. Leading to it were rails upon which a small trolley must have operated, supplying the catchers with harpoons and other necessities for their sea hunts. Standing behind the right side of the pier were huge oil storage tanks, each one as large as a full gasometer. Near to the factory buildings were large warehouses which had stored all kinds of whaling equipment, and lying around were the remains of many jute bags which had once held whale bone meal. Standing apart was a large boiler house which had supplied steam and electricity for the factory buildings and for heating the living quarters of the men. There was also a well equipped hospital which consisted of two wards with fifteen beds, an operating theatre, a first aid room and a bathroom which had showers as well as a long bath. On a wall in one of the wards hung a frame in which was a message to say that everything had been left for any sailors who had to seek shelter because of an emergency.

Outside the factory, up on a small hill, stood a red-painted house, which had been the residence of the British Magistrate, whose duty was to maintain law and order, and to keep a careful check on everything which was manufactured on the island, as the company had to pay a percentage levy to Britain. In front of the house still stood the white pole upon which the Union Jack had been hoisted.

Another house had been built nearby, and it too, had its flag-pole. Here would have been hung the Norwegian flag, for in this white house had lived the representative of the Norwegian whaling company with his wife. We had the feeling that they were still there to greet us, as on the walls hung some pictures of themselves with different views of the island as background.

Back in the factory we visited the main recreational building. It was named the Town Hall, and we were surprised to find a stage set with scenery. In a small room behind the stage were stored a piano and an altar, so the hall must have been the church on Sundays. Men who liked to read and study were well catered for, as bookshelves lined the walls, while tables and chairs still sat where they had been left, grouped for quiet study.

Behind the factory and the towering mountains we found what was probably the most southerly graveyard in the world. It was pathetic in the extreme to read the inscriptions on the stones which had been made in Norway and sent south by the whaling ships when they returned from leave. I even read an inscription from a bereaved wife who lived in my native town of Larvik.

Beyond the graveyard and still further away from the factory stood a black painted shed in which we found cases of gun powder and time fuses for use in the firing of harpoons.

Later, nearer the water, we were intrigued to find many wells of fresh water. Each one was covered with a roof upon which was written the name of a ship; so it appeared that each ship had its own private supply of fresh water. Before we departed we were glad to replenish our tanks with this beautifully clear water.

We remained a week in this harbour, and I returned several times to study more closely the buildings as well as the general construction of the town. Names had not been invented, but were taken from familiar home places. Thus the avenue leading to the Magistrates house was called Whitehall Street, while the path leading to the white house of the Norwegian representative, was called *Storgaten*—(High Street). At the turntable for the little trolley railway, there was a notice saying Kjose junction, but at usual stopping places the notice only gave the name of a station, called after a railway halt of Vestfold in Norway, the district where most of the whalers came from.

There must have been an earthquake in the vicinity after the whalers had departed, because I found a large floating dock lying far up on the beach. The pillars upon which the oil storage tanks stood were damaged, and one of the tanks was lying over on its side. Many of the concrete foundations of the buildings were cracked, and the windows of one of the hospital wards had been blown in, so that snow had piled high, covering the beds. We did what we could to barricade the windows with the wood which we found lying around, so that no more snow would blow in, and the place could be used again if necessary.

After visiting the graveyard I kept wondering why so many of the men working there had died young; therefore after we had cleared the snow from the hospital and put it to rights again, I searched about for some clues which might explain the cause of the deaths. Tucked away inside a locker, was a copy of a log book in which all sicknesses and deaths were registered. The reason given in most cases was "By accident at work". One 19-year-old youth had been attempting to climb some of the volcanic rocks when he had slipped and was killed.

I found evidence everywhere that the station had had other inhabitants after the whalers had gone. RATS! There must have been thousands and thousands of them, although I saw none, either dead or alive. Nothing had escaped the jaws of those rodents. Even the marks of their gnawing was visible inside the discarded whale bones. Carpets which had been neatly rolled and stacked on shelves were practically reduced to powder. Only tinned foods had defeated them.

The shelter of the harbour and the facilities of the station afforded us the opportunity of taking the *Polar Star* ashore to assemble it and prepare it for flight. Every day we worked on the plane, and when ready it was hoisted back on board, this time completed with propeller, wings, and mounted on skis.

On the morning of 12th December we made preparations for leaving. Yet I could not get out of my mind the picture of that lonely graveyard; it was too sad to leave my countrymen lying there so far from home, so two hours before we left I returned alone to that forlorn spot, taking with me a Christmas Begonia plant which I had bought in Bergen. I placed it right in the middle of the cemetery in respect to those who lay there, and as my little Christmas gift to them all.

Before reaching the ship I had to turn my head once more in the direction of the gravestones and there shining like a bright red jewel set on white velvet, was the little Christmas Begonia plant. I was glad that I had returned to make that gesture, and only then I felt that I was free to leave the island.

CHAPTER EIGHT

The Ross Sea

We left the little pier at noon, dipping our flag, and giving three
hoots on the ship's siren in farewell. Again we had to plough our
way back through the ice of the harbour, then through the
narrow entrance and out to open water. We set our course south-
westerly to follow the coast of Graham Land for the Ross Sea.

Early next morning, in 63° 50′ S. and Longitude 62° 40′
W., we passed two very strange rocks named the Portuguese,
so called because each rose from the sea exactly like a sail of a
Portuguese sailing boat.

Lying off Palmer Land there is an island called Adelaide
Island, and soon after passing it we spotted Alexander First
Island, which was discovered by the Russian Captain Bellinghausen in 1819 and at that time he believed it to be part of the
mainland. The sea through which we sailed was named after
Captain Bellinghausen, as it was the region in which he had
done most of his explorations.

Further south, we sailed into Amundsen Sea on Christmas
Day. The weather was changing all the time; a sunny spell
was soon followed by fog, which in turn changed to snow, then
back to sunshine again. We began to encounter large whaling
ships in 120° 00′ W. Evidently the whales inhabiting this
region had not yet been killed out or scared away, as those
around Deception Island had been.

One sunny day in early January 1934, when there was very
little swell on the sea, we came close to a large whaling ship
which was flying the South African flag. It was called the
Tafelberg after Table Mountain, which towers over the city of
Capetown, the ship's home port. After saluting each other, we
went alongside the *Tafelberg*, with a big whale lying between
us acting as a buffer.

50

A ladder was sent down from the ship to us and we were invited to come on board. I felt that I was back in Vestfold again, as on board, all the whalers came from Larvik, Sandefjord, and Tönsberg.

We were invited to inspect the whole process of whale dissection. First, the whale was dragged from the sea over a slipway aft to be flenched on deck. Then the blubber, which can be up to 18 inches thick, was removed and hoisted aloft on the derricks by a windlass, sliced and dropped into a perforated drum; this was rotating in a steam boiler, to reduce the blubber to oil. The liquid mixture of oil and water was then emptied into a separating machine to obtain the pure oil while the water residue was pumped into the sea.

After the blubber had been removed from the carcass, a second windlass dragged it to the forepart of the flenching deck, where the meat was removed from the bones, and processed in the same way as the blubber. The skeleton was then dissected into hundreds of pieces of large bone saws, and put through a grinder before it was subjected to the boiling process; this became bone meal. Only the intestines were rejected; otherwise, every part of the whale was used.

Certain whales were protected from slaughter: these were the pregnant animals, those which were suckling their young, and young animals under 60 feet long. If a whale of under 60 feet was harpooned by mistake, each member of the catcher crew forfeited his bonus, and the company had to pay a fine. Every whaling ship carried two international control officers to keep strict supervision on this.

If a fin-back of 70 feet was caught, the meat was cleaned, and put into deep freeze to be sold as food. A ready market was found for this delicacy in Japan, which sent special refrigerated ships to collect it. Some of the meat from the larger animals was kept back from the boiling processes to be sold in Europe as animal food—particular to fox and mink farms. It was reckoned that each foot of the total length of a whale would yield a barrel of oil, accordingly from a 90-foot whale ninety barrels of oil could be expected.

Attached to the stern of the factory ship and floating in the water, were about forty whales which had been delivered from the catching ships. Every tail was marked by the ship which had harpooned the whale to indicate the men who were entitled to the bonus accrued from it.

Before proceeding on our voyage, we accepted an invitation to go out on one of the catching ships, leaving some of the crew to look after the *Wyatt Earp* during our absence. We had not sailed far when we spotted the blow of a whale. It was then "full speed ahead" in the direction of the animal; as we approached it, the gunner ran forward to stand by the harpoon gun, but he waited until the ship was about 50 metres from the whale before firing. It was a good shot, and the whale was killed instantly. The rope attached to the harpoon was then pulled in by a windlass and after the whale was chained securely along the ship, air was pumped into the body, just below the skin, to keep it afloat.

After the catch had been delivered to the factory ship, we reboarded the *Tafelberg* before returning to our little ship, and as we bade farewell to the crew, they presented us with fresh eggs, meat, fruit and vegetables. As a surprise, we even had reconstituted milk from a contraption which they called "The iron cow".

Soon after we had left the *Tafelberg*, we picked up radio signals from another whaling ship which was lying further west in the Ross Sea. When we contacted it to enquire about the weather conditions in that vicinity, the reply was "Gale to storm, snow, and drifting icebergs". This was certainly no encouragement to proceed, but as we had already weathered many fearsome storms, we decided to keep on course, heading for Biscoe Bay and King Edward VII Land, where we hoped that we could make a landing. After battling our way through ice and snow, we reached the entrance of Biscoe Bay and discovered, to our dismay, that it was completely blocked by ice. However, we managed to sail close to Cape Colbeck on King Edward VII Land, although the pack ice prevented our approaching the barrier. Even the Bay of Whales was blocked, and we had no other alternative but to sail on to Ross Island in the hope of making a landing there. On 22nd January, we came close to the island, but as the drifting ice threatened to block us in, we were compelled to sail outwards from the barrier again. It was then that we managed to get a glimpse of the two extinct volcanoes on Ross Island, Mount Terror and

Mount Erebus, but their tops were obscured by rising mist.

To return to open waters again, we had to steer a more northerly course. In doing so, we approached Franklin Island where we stopped and moored the ship on the southern end of the island. We hoped that here we would find a suitable take-off place for a flight, but once again we were prevented from making any survey by the unbelievably bad weather conditions. After waiting four days for the blizzard to die down, we set sail again with our course following the coast of south Victoria Land, hoping to land at Cape Adare.

CHAPTER NINE

Home of the Elephant Seals

On 3rd February we sighted the giant volcano, Mount Sabine, which is over 10,000 feet high. We knew then that we could not be far from Cape Adare.

We rounded the Cape the following day and entered Robertson Bay. This bay was free from drifting ice on the eastern side, and as the wind was coming from a south-easterly direction we moored the ship to the ice shelf, although flight was quite out of the question by then. We kept up radio contact with various whaling ships, and from each we were informed about the weather conditions in the area in which it was stationed. From these reports, together with our own observations from weather balloons, we worked out our weather charts; every four hours we sent up weather balloons, selecting the size and colour according to the visibility at the time.

As we were well past the Antarctic midsummer, we had to make frequent checks on the temperature of the water, as well as paying constant attention to wind direction and pressure. We were soon to see the first warning signs of the coming of the Big Freeze. These were the ice plates—large discs about two inches thick which had begun to shoot up from the bottom of the sea. This phenomenon is caused by a stream of ice cold water sweeping over the sea bed, causing patches of water to freeze suddenly and rise to the surface. The appearance of these discs not only act as a warning to leave the area before the whole sea freezes, but their presence spells another, more imminent danger. When they reach the surface, they partly melt and break, forming fields of ice sludge which can penetrate and block up the intake to the engine's cooling system, causing damage to it and to the engine itself.

We did not leave the barrier immediately we spotted the ice

plates, because there were only a few and the temperature of the water surface was still above freezing point. Nevertheless, we were always on the alert, and only a small group of us went ashore at one time, leaving the others on the look-out. If these discs were to appear around us in all directions, the sea would become solid sludge, and the cold southerly wind from the barrier would complete the freezing operation.

As the ship lay in shelter we took the risk of landing on Cape Adare, because the inner bay had large patches entirely free from ice and snow. There lived thousands of seals, and a short distance away a colony of elephant seals. These great animals intrigued us so much, that instead of exploring the immediate vicinity, we spent some time studying them.

At one time they had been hunted for the large quantity of oil secreted in their bodies, with the result that in some areas they had become extinct. But it was obvious that these creatures had never seen humans before, because at first they made no effort to move, and did no more than glance at us until we dared to touch one of the females. This spurred the "lord of the harem" into action, and he lumbered towards us foaming at the mouth.

Sea elephants are extremely ungainly in their movements on land, and certainly no match for the agility of man. We took full and unfair advantage of that fact by giving him playful pokes with our ski sticks—we each carried one although we had left our skis behind on the snow—then by luring him away from his females in order to run back and stand in the middle of the herd. This particular herd had about sixteen cows, all very small compared with the bull, and we were able to lift one quite easily. The poor male's effort to return to the rescue at full speed, made him so exhausted that all he could do was to gaze at us balefully with no energy left even to blow out froth at us.

Thinking about our fun in retrospect, I have to admit that we were very unkind to the animal, because while we had been teasing him, several bachelor males had been watching the whole performance from the water. As soon as we moved away, they came ashore to take full advantage of our victim's exhausted state; he lost the fight and had to take to the water to lick his wounds.

As we were in the region in which my hero, Captain Borch-grevink, had wintered, I asked one of the Americans to accompany me in search of some evidence. We set out by ski with our rucksacks well stacked with food, a thermos flask with hot coffee, and other necessities, lest a blizzard blow up and we should be stranded. From the ship we had spotted further in the bay a large mound upon which there was no snow. We made this our target, and reached it after ski-ing for $2\frac{1}{2}$ hours. This mound turned out to be a mass of great volcanic rocks upon which there was not even a flake of snow. From these rocks to the sea level—about 50 metres—was an area of very fine sand. In it, immediately next to the rocks, was a well which had obviously been constructed by man. It was about 4 to 5 feet wide and 6 feet deep. Inside, stones had been piled neatly and these, together with the sand, had filtered the water from the melting snow beyond the volcanic rocks, thus producing clear drinking water. This must surely have been the source of fresh water for the men of the *Southern Cross*. Nearby, we noticed steam rising from some of the rocks which we discovered to be very hot. Even in some patches of the sand we found extreme heat when we buried our hands in it up to wrist level.

We sat down on these warm rocks turning our faces towards the sun while we ate our sandwiches and drank our hot coffee, comparing our lot with the old explorers who had never heard of a vacuum flask, let alone a transmitter for keeping up communication with the ship. Here, we could even call up the wireless operator on the ship and ask him to relay news from the outside world. The *Southern Cross* had not even a ship's radio, for it was not until at least six years after she had wintered off Cape Adare, that radio communication between ships, and from ship to shore, had been introduced.

Refreshed by our food and hot coffee, we continued to investigate in all directions from the well, but we were unable to discover any other evidence of previous exploration.

We returned to the spot where we had left our skis, and after fitting them on again, we made a little detour as we set off on the return journey. We headed for the plateau which overlooked the Ross Sea, and on reaching it, we looked down to see our little ship *Wyatt Earp* nestling in the shelter of Robertson Bay. Turning away again from the direction of the sea, we were attracted by a grey shining substance which protruded through some of the ice patches. We went to investigate, and on chipping away the ice, we found granite. These rocks, of varying sizes, must have been brought to this place millions of years ago by the action of the ice, and they were still visible due to the heat from the nearby volcanic rocks, which had melted the snow and ice surrounding them. Some of the other rocks which were exposed had the unbelievable appearance of having been painted. When we examined these stones carefully, we found mosses of various colours. This indeed was a mystery, and we wondered if the skuas and petrels had brought the spores on their feet, for in the hollows of the nearby rocks were scores of empty shells of eggs laid by these great birds which had departed before the long Antarctic winter had set in.

I learnt that the scientists of Byrd's 1934 expedition discovered that these small plants are frozen for most of the year round, but spring to life in the few hours of sunlight which last for only a week in the year, but which is sufficient to enable the minute mosses to maintain their hold on the rocks.

Pausing to have a final look round before making the ski run down to the ship, I could not help comparing the utterly desolate picture of the freezing sea beneath us and of the urgent necessity to leave the area at once, with the places which I had visited in the same latitude in the northern hemisphere. There, not only were there many species of wild life which could not have survived in the Antarctic, but whole cities, such as Hammerfest and Tromsö, where the long dark winter days do not impede the inhabitants as they go about their daily work.

We had been away from the ship for about nine hours, but we reckoned that the trip had been well worth the effort. I should have been most disappointed to have come so close to the spot where Borchgrevink and his party had wintered without searching to find some relic of the *Southern Cross* expedition. Although the well was the only evidence which we could find, it gave us the clue regarding the place where the ship had been beset by the ice and screwed up for a whole winter.

CHAPTER TEN

Winter in Dunedin

On 11th February the temperature of the water round the ship had dropped considerably, and ice discs were appearing all over the bay. We respected Nature's warning, and made preparations for leaving. During the evening, we made radio contact with the British ship *Discovery II* which was in the Ross Sea at 71° 00′ S. and 145° 00′ W. Her report was that the ice conditions were extremely bad, and it was obvious that flight from the Ross Sea to the Weddell Sea was quite impossible; but we still hoped to investigate the variations in the sea currents around the Ross Sea before leaving the Antarctic for the winter months.

Setting out from Robertson Bay the following morning we steered our course in an easterly direction, continuing until we encountered large pack ice. As our past experiences of pack ice had made us extremely wary of its dangers, we held a meeting to decide whether or not we should try to force a passage through it. The consensus of opinion was that we should alter course in order to keep to open water as much as possible. There was a gale blowing from a south-easterly direction, causing the pack ice to drift northwards, and we were compelled to alter course many times. All hope of exploration in the Ross Sea was now gone, but we continued to keep up radio communication with other ships, and to record our own observations in order to complete our daily weather charts.

Ten days after leaving the shelter of Robertson Bay, we discovered that we had been forced back to 70° 00′ S. and 180° 00′ W. Thus on 21st February, we knew that we had no alternative but to head north for Dunedin to winter there. Our course was set to take us past Scott Island, but there was a haze over the sea as we approached its position, and as we were surrounded by so many giant icebergs, we could not identify the island. By measuring some of those giant bergs with our sextants, we discovered that their heights ranged from 100 to 450 feet. We gauged their lengths by the speed of the ship as we passed them, and found that several of them were about 25 miles long! Nevertheless, although we could not claim actually to have seen Scott Island, we dipped our flag in salute to the great Antarctic explorer when we passed the charted position of the island which had been named after him.

We were then about to leave the Antarctic Circle, but we were were still in very grave danger from those ice sky-scrapers between which we had to wend our way. We did not dare to stop, as the force of the gale and sea would have dashed us against a berg, and a submerged ledge would have sliced through the bottom of our little craft. The situation was so menacing that at times we felt that it was impossible to survive the ordeal. In those days, there was no radar to help us to steer our way through the dense fog which had begun to envelop us; today many of these dangers are eliminated, as icebergs and other obstacles show up on the radar screen. In 1934, we had only to trust to our own instincts and keep going, with each man taking his turn so that a constant look out could be maintained.

It took us fully four days to come through the iceberg zone as the gale, which had veered round to north-westerly, brought us face to face with driving sleet and snow after having to contend with the fog. Even after sailing clear of the bergs, we still had to get through great fields of pack ice before we could feel safe.

Although each one of us was fully aware of the perils which surrounded us, there was never any panic on board, as we were all too intent on our duties, but at last we sailed into the safety of open waters in 56° 25' S. and 10° 00' E.

We were relieved to be heading for warmer weather again, and looked forward to respite from the extreme dangers of the Antarctic seas, but at the same time we had pangs of regret at having to leave the Southern Continent, as every day had brought us new adventures. I wished that I could have remained with the penguins and seals, to have had more time to study the rocks in the volcanic regions, and to have searched for fossils and signs of plant life, but I had to wait until we returned the following September, which is the beginning of spring in Antarctica.

Once more, I would have the thrill of beholding the south midnight sun light up the barrier as it glistens on the hard-packed snow. Many times I had seen the midnight sun in the north of Norway, but in the southern hemisphere it has an ethereal beauty of its own, particularly when the late light gleams on the distant icebergs, and colours each with a different fairy-like hue.

After our perilous winding passage through the towering icebergs, then our struggles in the vast areas of pack ice, and finally our return through the Roaring Forties, we safely reached calmer waters again as we approached South Island, New Zealand.

Before sighting land, we had informed the pilot station by ship-to-shore radio of our approach, and just as we sailed towards Dunedin Harbour we were met by the pilot launch. Dawn was breaking on 4th April 1934 as we slowly entered the harbour, and standing on the bridge of the *Wyatt Earp* I felt curiously fascinated to see once more tree-covered hill tops and large expanses of green fields.

The harbour pilot standing beside me shook his head in disbelief that such a small ship with only a handful of men could have come all the way from Norway via the Antarctic regions, and arrive in New Zealand entirely unscathed.

As we approached the breakwater, we were instructed to hoist a yellow flag, and to moor the ship alongside the quarantine shed as we had to be examined by the health authorities. The seaman on duty at the wheel laughed loudly. He was our ship's doctor, and of course he knew very well that we were no menace to the citizens of Dunedin, as we had come directly from the South Polar regions where sub-zero temperatures kill all germs and viruses which causes diseases. On our arrival, the examining authorities in their turn looked at the doctor and grinned. He was listed as "Doctor-Ordinary Seaman"!

Formalities over, the American members of the expedition prepared to leave us to rejoin their families in U.S.A., while we eight Norwegians remained to look after the *Wyatt Earp* and to have her ready for our next attempt at Antarctic exploration.

The arrival of our little wooden ship drew large crowds to the harbour as the *Wyatt Earp* had been given a great deal of publicity in the newspapers of the world.

A seamen's club called The Flying Angel invited us to make use of its facilities, and there we were surprised and delighted to be greeted by some fishermen in our own language. They had spotted the Norwegian flag at the stern of our ship, and were very anxious to meet us. We invited them to come and look over the *Wyatt Earp* and when they came aboard, they informed us that there was a Norwegian community established at Oban on Stewart Island, which lies south of the South Island. The original Norwegian settlers had once been whalers who had taken the opportunity of giving up that occupation when their ships had put in at Wellington for repair and supplies, as they had found the climate agreeable, and work easy to obtain. Some had taken to shark hunting (shark liver is used in some soaps), but most had returned to the occupation of their forefathers, fishing. Gradually, Paterson Creek had become the main harbour for a fishing fleet of small Norwegian fishing boats. Most of the men were second generation New Zealanders, but one or two had themselves been born in Vestfold, and I found myself in the centre of a group of these Norwegian New Zealanders who were anxious to find out about people whom they had known in their youth in Norway.

We held "Open Day" on Sundays, and hundreds of people accepted the general invitation to come aboard. Apart from the Norwegians, most of the other inhabitants of South Island were of Scots descent, and I noticed one curious feature which distinguished them from the people of other parts of Great Britain. They always referred to the land of their forebears as Scotland, while other settlers from Britain referred to England or Wales as "The Old Country" with a certain amount of nostalgia. The Scots were more matter-of-fact, and nothing seemed to please them more than to be greeted with "Hallo, Scottie!"

During the first few weeks of our sojourn we received several requests from schools to be allowed to bring parties of teenagers to the ship for first hand knowledge about the

Antarctic. As my compatriots did not speak much English, I had to answer their questions, the most common one being: "Why do you have a wooden ship?"

Some boys offered their services in helping us prepare for our next expedition. We allowed them to come on board in relays armed with scrubbing brushes, dusters, paint brushes, and even needles and threads. One boy was very anxious to mend the sails and was very disappointed to learn that they were in perfect condition! We referred to these boys as "The Young Explorer's Club"—a title which thoroughly delighted them. Each evening after they had finished their work, they were rewarded by sharing our evening meal with us, on condition that they washed their own dishes afterwards, but as it prolonged their time aboard, they did that extra chore gladly. I must confess that we were more grateful for their kindly act in consuming our tinned food than we were for their efforts at painting.

Towards the end of May we began in earnest to repaint the ship's sides and retar the decks as well as giving the engine a thorough check. The *Polar Star* had also to be thoroughly inspected, cleaned and oiled, although it had never been out for flight; as there were still some months before we were due to depart, it had to be re-covered with paper.

I think that it was about the end of June I received a letter from the Naval Base giving me the unexpected news that I had been promoted to the rank of Lieutenant. During our Antarctic wanderings, I had made my own private log book of observations which I had taken, noting how they had differed from existing printed charts and maps. I had noted as well findings which had not been published, and which I believed would be of interest to my Commander and former class mates; so as soon as the *Wyatt Earp* had put into Dunedin, I had posted a long newsy letter to Horten. I had not intended it to be submitted as an official document, but evidently the Commander had not only been interested and pleased to receive it, but had decided that the contents had merited promotion before my return.

By the middle of August, the ship was in top condition, ready for the return of the other members of the expedition. Since there was little else that we could do until then, we just relaxed or went fishing in the harbour in one of the lifeboats which we also used on shore visits.

It was during those days of relaxation that my attention was drawn to divers who were working from a jetty. I crossed over to find out what they were doing. Apparently, their task was to prepare low exits for new sewage pipes, so that the contents thrown out would sink, and not pollute the harbour. One day they took with them a very large quantity of dynamite. A great explosion sent tons of water into the air, forming a giant water spout. I reckoned that if dynamite could not only remove submerged rocks but send so much water upwards, it might also be of service to us, should we find ourselves encased in the ice on our next attempt in the Antarctic. I decided therefore to make the suggestion to Sir Hubert Wilkins on his return.

I did not have long to wait, for it was Sir Hubert himself who was the first to come back. When I told him of my idea, he at once agreed to accompany me to the scene of the activities on the other side of the harbour. While we were there, we witnessed the last of the underwater blastings, after which giant pipes were lowered into the water. Sir Hubert turned to me and instructed me to add half a ton of dynamite to the equipment list. Commending me for my idea, he added, "Now I have another suggestion. After dynamite, write COMPLETE DIVING OUTFIT." I asked who would be the diver, and was taken aback at his reply. "Myself, if no one else volunteers."

We had both seen underwater explosions before, but here was our opportunity of learning at first hand about the amount of dynamite required at different depths. When we approached the supervisors for information, they and the divers were all very willing to give us the benefit of their own experiences.

By the end of August, the ehccking of provisions and equipment was completed, but we had to await the arrival of Mr Ellsworth and the other Americans before the order to load the ship was given. This took place about two weeks later, and soon barges plied back and forward from the various warehouses, laden with sufficient food, clothing and polar equipment to last us for another year.

After stacking everything into the appropriate compartments of the hold, we were all on deck relaxing, when we were surprised to see a little motor boat coming alongside. A mysterious box was then hoisted up. It so happened that I was the one to receive it, and as I stood looking at it, the little boat turned swiftly and chugged back to shore. At the sound of the engine died away, I began to hear strange noises coming from within the box itself. I wondered at first if the box contained a dog but by listening more intently I realized that the noises were the grunts of a pig!

The anonymous donor had sent the gift with kindly intentions, but the presence of a piglet presented problems. We held a meeting to decide what to do with the animal, and in the end concluded that we had no alternative but to keep it, as we had no means of returning it; since I had taken delivery of it, I was given the responsibility for its good behaviour.

She was a dear little thing, and in a way I was quite glad at the prospect of having a pet to keep me company during my off-duty spells. I measured her from her snout to the tip of her curly tail, made a rough calculation of her likely speed of growth, and then set about making a little home for her. Over the entrance I painted "Miss Piggy's Cottage".

As we were still in the harbour, we placed the kennel on the deck for her to sleep, but her cries were so pathetic that we agreed to allow her to sleep aft in the port corridor. This arrangement appeared to please her very much, but during the day she preferred company and followed us about like a little dog. In order to come from within the corridor on to the deck, she had to cross a high threshold. As this obstacle was much too high for little Piggie, one of the A.B.s made a ramp on each side of it to facilitate her passage on to the deck. Already the little thing was showing cleanly instincts, for it did not at any time foul the corridor but waited until she got outside on deck before obeying the call of Nature. But even this state of affairs could not be tolerated, and we took on ten bags of sawdust to make her a little private toilet in the corner of the deck. The engineer offered the engine room for stowing it to keep it dry and warm.

As the time drew near for our departure, we arranged to have the bottom of the ship checked. The *Wyatt Earp* was so small and the cargo so light, that she was hoisted up on the slipway by the harbour's windlass without any difficulty. No flaw or damage was discovered, but we remained there for two or three days for the removal of seaweed and barnacles.

During that time, I became aware of discussions going on between Mr Ellsworth, Sir Hubert Wilkins, Mr Balchen and the Captain, and somehow I felt that they concerned me. I was not held in suspense for long, for as soon as the ship had been taken off the slipway, I was informed that I was to become the first mate on the ship, while the senior of the two A.B.s, Mr Liavaag, would be promoted to be second mate. As the main purpose of the expedition was the flight across the Antarctic continent, it was essential that until it had taken place, Mr Balchen, the chief pilot, had to remain as relaxed as possible. He was therefore relieved of his duties as the first mate on the ship. Liavaag did not have papers in navigation, but he was a very experienced sailor who understood ice conditions, and without difficulty he assumed his new role.

Before setting out once more for the Antarctic, we had to make a trial run to ensure that the ship engine and rudder were in perfect condition, and as a reward for the help which they gave us during our months at anchorage in Dunedin Harbour, we invited the boys of "The Young Explorer's Club" to come aboard for the last time. They were thrilled and excited as we weighed anchor and sailed out of the harbour. Indeed they appeared to have as much pride in our little ship as we ourselves had. So it seemed most appropriate when some years later, I read that the *Wyatt Earp* had been sold to New Zealand as a training ship. I pictured the joy on the faces of the youngsters who had come out on the trial run, and wondered if they had ever returned to look at the old ship.

On our trials everything responded perfectly, and we were confident that our little ship was again capable of braving the perils of the great frozen waters. On the morning of 11th October 1934, our meat supply was delivered from shore, and as before, it was placed high up on the foremast rigging. That same night, after darkness had fallen, we slipped quietly out of Dunedin's Harbour with the course set for the Ross Sea.

CHAPTER ELEVEN

Stuck in the Pack Ice

It was good to be out in the open sea again, to hear the healthy, strong throb of the engine, and the wind soughing through the sails. The ship responded well after its long spell of inactivity, as she rose and fell with the waves.

I had the morning watch, and just as dawn was breaking, my eye caught the movement of something on deck. At first I thought that it was Piggy, but when I saw it jump from the deck on to the hatch, I realized that it was a cat, and I whispered "Pussy, pussy", to which the animal replied with a loud "Mi-aaow". I went down to the deck to pick it up, and found that it was a young grey tabby. How it came aboard was a complete mystery. I carried it back to the wheel-house with me to show it to the sailor on duty at the wheel. As we wondered what we were to do with it, the A.B. had a sudden inspiration. He reminded me that the heaviest sleeper aboard was the steward, and suggested that I should tiptoe to his cabin door and deposit the cat inside. At 6 a.m., the steward was called as usual, and seconds later we saw Pussy rushing across the deck being chased by the steward in his night attire.

When Sir Hubert Wilkins learned of the presence of Puss, he intimated that he hoped that the *Wyatt Earp* was not to be transformed into Noah's Ark!

However, the presence of the cat solved one great problem which so far had beaten us. The piglet had not yet taken the hint regarding the box containing the sawdust, and was still soiling the deck. Pussy understood its purpose at once, and as soon as Piggy saw the cat going towards it, she followed, and from then onwards, the deck remained clean.

The last piece of New Zealand territory which we saw was an uninhabited island of about 100 square miles named Campbell

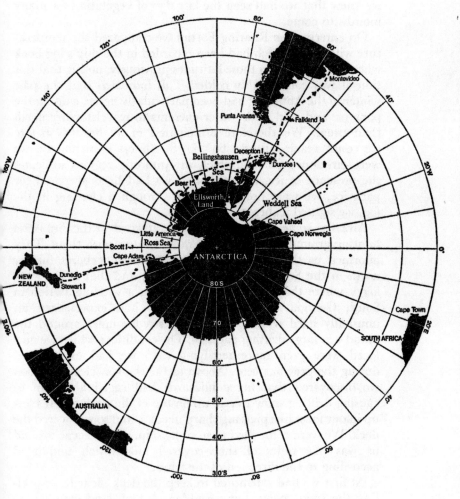

2. 1934–1935 Season

Island. As its wooded mountain disappeared from view astern, we knew that we had seen the last sign of vegetation for many months to come.

On entering the Roaring Forties we compared the temperature with those which had been recorded in the ship's log book when we had been in those latitudes previously, noting that this time it was considerably colder. This indicated that the past winter in the Antarctic had been particularly fierce, causing the pack ice and cold underwater currents to travel further north than usual. We therefore anticipated many hazards before we could reach latitude 60° 00′ S. Almost immediately, we were enveloped in fog, which in Antarctic regions indicates the presence of ice, and although we had been prepared for pack ice, we were horrified when, through a clearing in the fog, we sighted icebergs.

Already, some whaling ships had returned to the Antarctic hunting grounds, and we made radio contact with them. They informed us that they too had encountered icebergs further north in the South Atlantic than usual, and that it was very foggy where they were stationed. Later, a whaling station in South Georgia warned us that they had experienced an unusually hard winter, and in the sea for miles around the island was large drifting pack ice. The conditions which we now faced were even more terrifying than we had experienced during the previous year. Above us the sky was clear but soon we discovered that fierce blizzards had raged ahead of us causing drifting snow to pile up on top of the pack ice. It blew up in our faces like piercing sharp needles, and soon covered the deck. We were compelled to stop the ship, for the scene around us was like miles of snow-covered hills which undulated according to the direction of the wind.

At first we had attempted to keep the deck clear by shovelling the snow away, but a sudden gust of wind caused it to pile up so much that the ship was almost buried under it. We had to work frantically for our dear life, as well as to keep a passageway clear from the fore part of the ship to the after part, as the length of the deck separated the cabin accommodation from the mess room. We therefore spread a long canvas which measured about half the length of the deck, and working together in a line we shovelled the snow from the deck on to the canvas which was hoisted over the side by the ships derricks, to be emptied when it could hold no more snow. The walls of blown snow which encased the ship grew to such a height that without the windlass which lifted the derrick's load high above them, we would soon have been obliterated altogether.

The shovelling and hoisting operation had to be kept up until the wind subsided. In the swirling winds which are prevalent in polar regions, the freezing snow adheres to any object which bars its advance, and as the ship happened to be the largest obstruction, we became the centre of the enemy wind's activities.

With the engine silent, we had no electricity, and we had to depend on oil lighting and heating, besides melting the water in the fresh water tank. This was normally prevented from freezing by a coil in the tank heated from the engine. Our cabins were likewise deprived of heat, and we were glad to make the maximum use of the galley stove.

In spite of all our difficulties we did not neglect Piggy and Pussy. We placed the animals' W.C. box and Piggy's Cottage at the stern, and covered them over with canvas, and to keep the little cottage warm, we placed a mattress inside it. Then the engineer devised a heating system for the little enclosure; this consisted of an oil drum into which dripped sufficient oil from a little tank above, and leading from the stove he placed a narrow pipe so that the suffocating fumes would be conducted through a hole in the canvas to the air outside.

A further danger beset us. The thick ice surrounding us began to screw, causing our little ship to list over to the port side. Closer, and closer pressed the giant lumps of pack ice, each of them weighing from about 2 to 10 tons, until three of them gradually swung up to lie over against the ship's side. One ice "pillar" actually stood higher than the level of the boat deck, while only a few feet away a snow mountain had been formed, its peak reaching the height at which our meat store hung on the foremast rigging. We were so stuck that we could not even use dynamite to free ourselves, and as far as the eye could see, there was not the tiniest patch of open water.

As we were beset so soon after our departure, our oil storage tanks in the engine room were both too full to effect any alteration in ballast by pumping from one to the other. We therefore had to depend on the oil drums which were stacked on deck to balance the ship in the event of its being screwed up still further by the action of the ice. Before we could transfer any from the listing port side to the starboard side, we had to use a hammer and crowbar to chip away the ice which had completely encased them all. It took us a very long time before we could free even four barrels. Then we had to keep a passageway clear for rolling them from one side to another when the need arose. To make this possible we had to use a very large quantity of rock salt, which although it prevented the snow from freezing during the day, at night when the temperature fell so many degrees below zero, it froze into slippery rime itself, thus adding yet another hazard.

As we could not possibly take the risk of anyone falling and breaking a limb, we took the precaution of spreading ashes from the galley stove over the passageway in the mornings. When we found that the quantity was insufficient for the purpose, we had to sweep the chimney for soot, and even after scraping the last traces of exhaust from the funnel when the soot finished, it still seemed as if the ice would beat us.

Together we presented a sorry sight. We were like a gang of chimney sweeps, and our ration of fresh water was not sufficient to wash away the dirt, which was ingrained in our faces, necks, and hands. We gathered some of the loose snow and filled a barrel with it, but it was so dry that it took a very long time to melt, and then it yielded only a quarter of a pint of water. We had plenty of soap to use in salt water, but the pack ice was so thick we could not get access to any salt water.

By this time, we felt sure that we had encountered every possible difficulty, but we were wrong, for soon we were to be attacked by an army of fleas! This apparently is a common occurrence on polar expeditions. Even the doctor was swarming with them. To keep ourselves sane, we indulged in some fun; we invented a competition to see how many fleas we could pick out from our T-shirts within a set time. Each one of us put in 30 cents and the winner took the jackpot. This little diversion gave us pleasure and took our minds away from the extreme danger that we were in. I never won the jackpot because I was too disgusted to count more than 100 fleas, but I decided to devise something to annihilate the plague, or at least disperse the parasites from their present quarters on my person. I tried the experiment of sewing oakum threads into the armpits and waist areas of my garments. This worked like magic, for my fleas left me at once; following upon my success the other men applied the same tactics, causing the whole army of the invading parasites to retreat. But we all were smelling strongly of tar, although it was preferable by far to the discomforts caused by the infesting fleas.

This difficulty having been overcome, Pussy suddenly became extremely popular. I have always been very fond of animals, and whenever I had the opportunity, I used to pick up the warm little creature, and hold it inside my anorak, warming my hands as I stroked her fur. It was not long before everyone else followed suit, and Pussy spent her time being passed from within one anorak to another. The benefit was mutual, for in heating our cold bodies, she enjoyed the shelter. Piggy, however, was a poor miserable little creature during those days, as she could not follow us out on deck, and accordingly grunted her displeasure continually.

Mr Ellsworth gave the order that our sweetheart, "Miss Piggy", had to be destroyed. As no one could be prevailed upon to be the killer, I knocked on Mr Ellsworth's door, which was next to mine, and handed him the revolver, saying that he would have to do the job himself, as everyone else refused. Then I added, "If you kill Piggy, we will all abandon ship." Piggy got her reprieve, and Pussy's future was likewise assured.

Mr Ellsworth took the joke in good part, as he knew that no one could leave the ship. From then onwards, he became chief guardian of the animals, and it was obvious that he was becoming very fond of them both. Their presence in many ways helped us to keep up our courage when it could have been so easy to give way to despair.

Whenever the wind abated and the snow ceased to blow up, we took turns of climbing to the crow's nest to search the horizon for black spots. These would have indicated small patches of open water. An even more welcome sight would have been the presence of seals, in which case, we should have expected breaks in the pack ice. But during the first seven days of our imprisonment, we saw no sign at all of approaching release.

On the eighth day, at the breakfast table, I asked for a volunteer to accompany me on a long distance ski journey, in the hopes that we might see the signs that we were awaiting, at a distance from the ship. Although I addressed the whole company, I hoped fervently that it would be one of my fellow countrymen who would volunteer, not for the reason that I thought that the Americans lacked courage—that was far from my mind—but they had not the same experience in skiing in bad weather conditions, and on rough, sometimes brittle undulating ice. At first they looked at me as if our ordeals had somehow turned my mind, but I explained to my companions that my aim was to search for seal holes, as the animals had to be able to surface at frequent intervals in order to breathe, and they could do so only if there were breaks in the pack ice. At once, the second engineer, a Norwegian and an expert skier, offered to come with me.

Among our general equipment on board were four small coracle-like dinghies, so light that they could be stacked into each other. Now the occasion had come when we might have to use them. We placed one on a sledge, and inside, we loaded food, cooking utensils, an oil stove, a supply of oil and a tent. In case the going proved too hard for skis, we carried snow shoes. Then of course we had our radio transmitter, smoke flares and a gun. Should the ice crack suddenly, and we could neither use skis nor snow shoes for our return journey, we had the dinghy in which we could paddle our way back.

To prevent our losing sight of the ship, a large orange coloured flag was hoisted to the top of the foremast, and held out by a bamboo pole, so that it would continue to be seen if the wind should drop. We decided to try our luck first in a southerly direction, and to ensure our safety, we arranged with those left on board that whenever we came to the point when we could see no more than the flag on the horizon, we should release a flare, and they would do likewise in answer. After that, we planned to encircle the ship, at that radius.

The mid-day meal, which was almost ready, smelt very appetizing, but we had only a bowl of soup each before we set out, as it is not good to ski after a heavy meal. The load which we were to drag in turns weighed about 80 pounds, including the sledge. We planned that we should each pull it for a spell of half an hour at a time, while the other took bearings from the compass.

The scene from the ship had appeared to be relatively flat, but we were not far away when we realized that our progress would be slow as the ground below us was far from smooth; it was very rough and bumpy. After ski-ing for some three hours, we stopped to have some coffee, and, turning to face the ship, we realized that we had travelled already the length of the intended radius, for the flag at the top of the foremast rigging was barely visible through our binoculars. We therefore set off our smoke flares to indicate that we were about to begin our circling of the ship. A few minutes later, we saw the answering smoke signal rise. We reckoned that we had come a distance of $6\frac{1}{2}$ sea miles; the time was 3 p.m., but as we were in the spring of the Antarctic (when there is no real darkness) there was no need for us to hurry. We could therefore take our time to study the pack ice. So far, we had seen no sign of the presence of seals, not even the brown traces of their excrement. Most of the time it was difficult to believe that we were in fact ski-ing on water and not on *terra firma*, although occasionally we observed slight movement on the surface of the ice.

Above us, the sky was white as far as our eyes could see, and from our past experiences of the absence of black patches, we knew that the pack ice was continuous. At 8 p.m., we took bearings and found that the ship now lay east. We refreshed ourselves by eating fish balls, after which we ate prune compôte (from tins) and finished our meal with hot coffee and the steward's speciality—Danish pastries. After this meal, we continued on our way until 1 a.m., when we found that the ship now lay south-east. We were enjoying some good strong black coffee, and munching sandwiches when the ship's radio called us to ask when we intended to return, but we replied saying that we were having a splendid picnic and that we were in no hurry to return.

Had we told the truth, we should have informed them that we were very weary by this time, and stiff from the unaccustomed exercise; but as soon as we had stacked away our cups, we set course again for the ship. Although we had the same distance to travel as when we had set out, i.e. the $6\frac{1}{2}$ miles radius—it took us five hours this time, instead of three. We came aboard about 6 a.m., and after a good breakfast, we went to bed for the rest of the day. We set off again in the evening in a north-easterly direction with the ship on a west bearing. We had not gone far, when we began to notice a slight movement below our skis. Soon the wind began to freshen, but we continued until about 2 a.m., when the wind suddenly blew up fiercely, driving the snow against us like millions of tiny piercing needles and compelling us to cover our faces, leaving only our glasses exposed to protect our eyes.

We had now no alternative but to return to the ship, as we sensed the approach of a blizzard. The movement and crackling sound of the pack ice was becoming stronger and louder every minute. We now kept in continuous contact with the ship, for our companions on board confirmed what we had already felt, the loosening of the ice.

They promised to keep a constant look-out for us until our return, and mentioned that they had a lifeboat and life-saving gun at the ready, should the elements prove too strong for us. We knew from experience that it would take a long time before the pack ice would begin to part, yet we put a lifeline of 25 metres between us, in case one of us should slip into a crack. In this way there was an ample safety margin for the other to haul him out.

Breakfast was still in progress when about 9 a.m., we finally reached the ship in an exhausted condition.

We were back just in time, as about an hour after our return, a fierce blizzard blew up. The westerly storm, which at the same time had brought the beginnings of a thaw, had caused the water below the ice to move, and our little ship began to sway with the swell. This forced the sides to scrape against the heavy pack ice, which was working in a contrary movement to that of the water.

The storm was at one and the same time friend and a deadly foe. It had brought the first signs of the disintegration of the heavy pack ice, but with the thick driving wet snow, the visibility was reduced to nil. We did not dare start the engine until we could see the size of the ice lumps surrounding the ship, so the only alternative for us meantime was to hoist the fore and aft sails, to feel if it were possible at this stage for the ship to move forward at all. The sails acted first by giving us a slight list to port, then they steadied the ship by making it roll in the same rhythm as that of the heavy ice, which then ceased its crunching against our sides; but still we did not move one inch forward.

Nevertheless the sound of the flapping sails revived our spirits, as it was easy to imagine that we were sailing, in spite of our continued detention in the pack ice. Every minute the temperature was rising and thick snow flakes clung to the wire rigging, which soon assumed the dimensions of telegraph poles.

During our imprisonment in the ice, the refuse from the galley had been piling up round the sides of the ship and when we hoisted the sails, we used this as an indicator to see whether or not we were actually moving. When fresh snow obliterated all traces of the refuse, we had to resort to bamboo sticks which we projected from the ship's sides. An alteration in the angle would denote movement.

It was on the twelfth day that we began to realize that the ice was at last breaking up, because water started to seep into the intake to the cooling system of the engine. This allowed us to start the dynamo, which gave us the luxury of electric light in the corridors. It seemed very bright after all those days when we had to recourse to oil lamps. We were all excited now as it surely could not be long before we could get on our way again.

The following day, the thirteenth day of our incarceration, we observed sufficient water between the ice floes to effect a narrow channel. It was now safe to hoist the mainsail, and, at long last, we made our first forward movement, inch by inch, to escape from the rigours of the ice prison which had held us fast for thirteen days and nights.

Although we had begun to move, by the next day we had made very little headway because of the poor visibility. We had to rely entirely on our sails for most of the time, as until we could see at least 50 metres ahead, we did not dare use the engine for fear of damage to the propeller. Frequently when there had been a clearing and we had started the engine, we had to stop it again almost immediately. In the thick blizzard, many times without realizing it we sailed into a patch of open water when the ship suddenly gathered momentum and we were thrust head-on into the ice, the impact causing the ship to judder violently and uncontrollably. To avert catastrophe during further periods of blind sailing, we restarted the engine in reverse, as soon as the snowstorm abated, and we could see clear water again. This action together with the use of the sails acted as a brake, and from then on we hit the ice gently.

CHAPTER TWELVE

Seals, Birds and Whales

We were back to sea routine at last, and Pussy returned to her favourite haunts, the wheel-house and the chart room. In the wheel-house, she spent most of her time on the shoulder of the A.B. on duty, but when I was on watch, she jumped over to my shoulder whenever I moved close to the window. One day, she suddenly became excited and craned her neck forward and began sniffing, after which she jumped down and ran to the door.

I let her out, and watched her jump up on the life-belt box which was her best vantage point for looking over the side. Her sniffing became almost frantic, and catching the direction of her gaze, I recognized the unmistakable traces of seals, their brown excrement marks. These were very welcome signs indeed, and thanks to our little stowaway cat which had given us the clue, we realized that we were sailing into safer waters in which the ice was not so hard packed.

Nevertheless, we were destined to be ice-bound many times before we reached the Great Ice Barrier again. One day, during a spell when we had been forced to a stand-still, I heard from the distance the sounds of birds. Suddenly, a great flock of snow pigeons appeared over the horizon, flying from a south-westerly direction. I had observed these birds many times during our previous wanderings, but I had never been able to find out what their source of food was.

Here was my opportunity to study them, for it was obvious that we would not be able to move for some time. The sun was shining that day, and taking advantage of the good visibility, I climbed up to the crow's nest to watch the birds through my binoculars. Just as I was getting them into focus they began to fly round in a circle screeching excitedly. Suddenly, they swooped low over a patch of clear water around which seals lay on ice floes, sunning themselves. For a few minutes, the birds, after flying upwards, again kept swooping down, and it was obvious to me that they were trying to attract the attention of the seals to the water. Focusing the binoculars on the water, I could make out a patch of red. It was obviously a colony of plankton which was floating on the surface. The seals obeyed the signals from the birds at once, and dived to devour the tiny shrimp-like creatures, afterwards returning to their floes to rest after their meal. Like small boys who overeat at parties, they threw up the surplus food which their stomachs could not contain. Immediately, the hovering pigeons dived to partake of the rejected plankton.

The birds in their turn were just as greedy as the seals had been, and the weight of their meal prevented their being able to rise again, and they became easy prey for the seals which set upon them after their fill of plankton had been digested.

Sleep soon overcame the seals and they were therefore oblivious to the arrival of several skuas and petrels which had been hovering about for some time. They had arrived on the scene to devour the skins and general remains of the pigeons.

I smiled to myself as I looked at those great overfed seals through my binoculars, for little did they know that before long one of them was destined to provide a meal for us!

When I descended from the crow's nest I marvelled at Nature's methods of providing for her creatures, which must depend on each other's co-operation for food.

While thus musing, I was unaware of the presence of the steward who had come out on deck to draw my attention to the fact that the meat store on the rigging was almost finished, and suggested that we reserved the remainder for our main meal on Sundays, while we had the opportunity to kill one of the seals for eating. Our two A.B.s, who had had considerable experience in the Arctic as seal hunters, volunteered to go overboard to kill one of the animals. Most of them were asleep, and the others paid little heed to our presence. Therefore it was quite simple to approach them, and having selected his victim, one of the A.B.s killed it with a deft knock behind its ear, using a wooden hammer.

The two men then dragged the body to the side of the ship

for dissection. Acting upon the instruction of the steward, only the meat from the thigh was to be brought aboard, and the remainder left to the "vultures" of the frozen south, the skuas. Unfortunately, these vicious birds decided that they were to have the whole animal, because no sooner had the knife been inserted into the body, than scores of them swooped down to the attack and the A.B.s had to clamber aboard to safety, leaving the birds to devour the seal. In minutes all that was left was the bare skeleton. Having tasted blood, they kept swooping low over the deck until we were all in danger of attack. Some of the birds attempted to get at our precious meat on the rigging, but fortunately it was frozen so hard, and covered with such a thick layer of ice, that even their great beaks could not penetrate.

We tried to scare the birds away, first with sticks and brooms, and when that failed, someone fired a rifle, but the crack could not be heard above the noise of the birds. For the time being, we were compelled to retreat from the deck to the wheel-house and behind the portholes, until the skuas lost interest and flew off.

Soon after this episode, we found that it was possible for the ship to proceed a short distance, and at the next enforced halt, a second attempt was made to procure seal meat. This time, we erected a canvas shelter on the deck, as a protection against the birds, as it was obvious that the animal would have to be brought on board for dissection. As soon as the body was slit, the skuas returned, at once covering the canvas, the deck, and even the wheel-house, imprisoning those who were in it. I was fortunate in being off duty at the time and watched the scene from the windows of the galley. Everyone on deck was in danger of being attacked, as the smell of fresh blood drove the birds frantic. As a temporary measure of defence, smoke flares were thrown until the dissection was completed, and the unwanted parts of the carcass thrown overboard. The birds immediately swooped to finish off the remains of the seal, but again they returned to the deck which by this time was covered with frozen blood. It was quite interesting to watch their antics at this point. They strutted about the deck bending over to scoop up the blood "rime" on to their chest feathers. As soon as they had absorbed as much as possible, they flew down on to

79

the ice to savour the blood as they stripped it from the feathers. Nature has endowed these great birds with a mechanism which removes salt from the frozen water, and so provides them with fresh drinking water, and in this case, fresh blood.

The noise of the skuas and the smell of blood had attracted the cat which appeared on the deck amid the general confusion, but as she also became an object of attack, she had to retreat at great speed to hide under the windlass where she was forced to remain until she was rescued. After that day, Puss was extremely wary of Antarctic birds, and never again ventured out on deck alone.

Beneath her sheltering tarpaulin, Piggy's grunts rose in an aggressive crescendo. She was furious because she could not get out to see what was going on, but as soon as the danger was over, I went to pacify her with a tin of sweet milk, and her better nature was restored.

During another of our enforced halts in the pack ice on the way to the barrier, I decided to try another experiment. On previous occasions when I had had the opportunity of studying seals, I had noticed that they always slept on their stomachs, never on their backs. At first I could not think of a reason for this, as when they were awake, they sometimes turned on to their sides. Our recent experiences with the skuas made me wonder if the face-down position for sleeping was in order to protect their eyes, and I therefore decided to do a little acting in order to find out if this was the case.

I asked some of my companions if they would co-operate with me by standing by to come to my assistance should I be attacked by the skuas, which were now never far away from the ship, and threatened to be a hindrance in our future explorations. So when the next lot of them came to hover over the ship, I deliberately walked over the deck towards them. Although they circled round me, they made no attempt to attack. I then climbed on to the hatch and lay face downwards. But they still only encircled me at a distance. When I turned to lie on my back, at once a couple of giant birds swooped down to my face, in the nick of time, my companions succeeded in beating them off, and I jumped to my feet, a little shaken.

This attempt by the skuas to attack me without provocation made it all the more essential that we should learn when we ourselves were likely to be vulnerable, because on such an expedition, the members must at times separate and work alone. Accordingly I suggested that we continue our experiment on the ice which surrounded the ship. I began by walking about alone, while the others stood by observing the behaviour of the birds which again circled round me without flying too close. Then when I lowered myself into a crouching position, the birds flew lower, but still made no attempt at attack until once more I lay down on my back. At lightning speed they swooped down on me, and it was with great difficulty that my companions succeeded in beating them off until I could rise. I experimented no further! But we had learned that in spite of our glasses, our eyes and even our whole bodies were vulnerable to attack from these great birds, should we fall and be unable to rise without assistance. Now I knew without any doubt why the seals lay with their faces to the ground when asleep, and what had caused some of them to lose an eye. In fact several times after this experiment, I was saddened to witness skuas attack baby seals while their mothers were in the water hunting for food. The method was always the same, the eyes were first gouged out and swallowed, then the poor little maimed and helpless creature was greedily consumed in minutes.

At last we appeared to be approaching larger patches of open water, because were able to proceed for longer distances at a time than had been possible for several weeks.

One day, after we had passed through a lake of open water, we tried to plough our way through a patch of ice sludge, but it was thicker than we had anticipated, and we came to a standstill with our bow projecting into the ice while the stern was in open water. As the engine was silent, the mechanic who happened to be on duty at the wheel at the time took the opportunity to relax for a moment, with his arms resting between the projections on the wheel. Suddenly the wheel began to spin violently, and he was pitched first to the side of the wheel-house against the windows, which were shattered at the impact, and then flung back on the floor, unconscious, with one of his arms broken.

At first no one could understand what had happened, until two Hump-backed whales, a male and a female, emerged from below the ship. They were covered with whale lice, and had been rubbing themselves against the bottom of the ship in an attempt to get rid of the parasites.

The injured mechanic did not remain unconscious for long, and was able to go unaided in search of the doctor who was, at the time, off duty as a seaman. This was the doctor's first opportunity to act in his professional capacity, and very soon the injured man was patched up sufficiently to return to complete his spell of duty at the wheel. As the whales were still lying close to the ship, we decided to secure the wheel in order to prevent the rudder from being reduced to matchwood, should the animals resume their rubbing antics again. It was fortunate that we had taken this precaution, for although it seemed as if they were content merely to lie and gaze up at us, they suddenly darted below the ship again rocking us violently as they did so. The whales had no evil intent towards us, but were like a couple of playful children with a new toy. From time to time they lay on their backs making noises which sounded suspiciously like laughter, while they flapped their long flippers up and down, obviously enjoying themselves as the water splashed up the sides of the ship.

Although we managed to get the ship underway again, admittedly very slowly, the whales continued to keep us company by following us in the channel which the ship cut through the ice. Someone tried to scare them away by throwing the sounding line overboard at them, but this action merely added to their enjoyment, as they responded with some more chortling noises. It was quite obvious that the *Wyatt Earp* was the best toy that ever come their way, and they were enjoying it to the full. They continued to follow us until the novelty wore off, when they suddenly disappeared in search of a new diversion. Many times afterwards we recalled this interlude with the hump-backs, referring to it as our "Visit to the circus".

We continued to plough our way through the ice sludge, this time for about five hours before contact with thicker ice compelled us to come to a standstill. During that time, we had observed that ahead of us lay larger patches of open water, as in the far horizon the sky was black. When at length we reached this great stretch of open water, we were able to proceed without any fear of destruction by ice for at least two watches—approximately ten hours. During our passage through this great lake, we had to stop the engine occasionally for a few minutes at a time, not because of ice, but because of the presence of large areas of red plankton, which was floating on the surface of the water. As we could not avoid its being sucked into the intake to the cooling system, we could only stop the engine, then blow the pipe free with compressed air. These minor hindrances did not perturb us, for as well as the presence of the plankton, we had observed many blows of the giant fin-back and blue whales, a sure indication that we were at last coming to the end of the pack ice.

Sir Hubert Wilkins announced suddenly that he was going to take a little trip in the scouting plane, which was on deck completed with pontoons and therefore ready to take off from the water. The plane was lowered and he set off. When he returned after half an hour, he reported that as the horizon was white for miles around we should not be too optimistic. He added, however, that there was a large black stripe in the sky to the south. The plane was then refuelled, and Bernt Balchen took off to encircle the ship. He reported that there was a large number of whales in the vicinity, and remarked that the little plane was in perfect condition. After a further refuelling, I took my first trip in it. It was a delightful little plane to handle, and I enjoyed piloting it; in some ways, it reminded me of the naval exercises when I had to go off in search of lurking submarines. Looking down into the dark water below, I could easily imagine that I saw submarines, but these were the arching backs of the whales as they devoured their plankton diet. I was not quite prepared for the shock of seeing one of the whales fire a torpedo—at least that is what it appeared to do—and to make sure that I was not suffering from hallucinations, I flew low over the surface of the water and discovered that the group of whales below me were females, and the "torpedoes" were the baby whales setting out to experiment in swimming alone without the help of their mothers.

It was extremely interesting and amusing to watch those giants devour their food. The process resembled a huge vacuum cleaner at work. Each time one of those massive jaws opened, tons of water and plankton were drawn in, then as the mouth closed, from either side there emitted a froth such as appears when a bottle of champagne is freshly opened. This froth temporarily pushed aside the plankton which was still floating but which was immediately sucked into the mouth as the great jaws reopened.

After about twenty minutes in the air, I returned to land on the water beside the ship. The plane then was brought back on board and secured in its position on the afterdeck.

Although the ship was not beset by ice, but was lying in the vast lake within the ice-field, we were held up for about four hours until a small but necessary repair to the engine was completed. This gave most of us the opportunity to study the whales into whose territory we had intruded. We were particularly interested in one large female blue whale which we watched for a long time through our binoculars. It was swimming slowly and rather ungainly, as from time to time it turned over to its right side. After some time it came quite close to the ship, and we were able to observe that tucked under its left flipper was a very young baby whale. The rolling movement of the mother had been to allow the baby to breathe. By further patient observation, we were rewarded by witnessing the baby being fed. When it sucked its mother's milk, it rose partially out of the water. The mother, to facilitate the baby's sucking, lay round almost on its back, thus revealing that it had two teats, situated at the base of the stomach, each proruding from the body about a foot in length. As soon as the baby was satisfied, the mother grasped it with its left flipper again and held it close to her own body, and resumed the rocking movements. As the baby was tiny compared to the giant mother, I wondered if unless closely guarded at this stage of development it would fall prey to the larger species seals.

There were also many young adult whales swimming about, and at first I thought that they were playing some kind of game, until I realized that they were in pairs, male and female, and were going through a form of courtship. They approached each other at great speed, colliding head-on before rising together with their bodies half out of the water. As they fell backwards they parted, and taking opposite directions, they each completed a circle before hurtling head-on towards each other once more, with force sufficient to propel themselves out of the water with their stomachs against each other. This manœuvre was repeated many times before they swam away in the same direction.

After the repair to the engine had been completed, we got under way again, but we still had several more days of struggling through the ice before at last we sighed the barrier, and came out into open water, in which a few icebergs were drifting. It gave us all a thrill to sight Cape Adare once more. In all, it had taken us 65 days from the time we had left Dunedin to the time when we sighted South Victoria Land. During that time we had been 45 days in heavy pack ice and of that period 13 days at a complete standstill; but the sight of land again put our troubles behind us and we were ready for more adventures.

CHAPTER THIRTEEN

Second Christmas in Antarctica

We passed Mount Sabine on 18th December 1934, and it was a great surprise to discover that everything had changed since we had left that area ten months before. During that time, a new ice barrier had been formed, so extensive that it now encompassed several small islands which we had noted the previous year, thus making them appear to be part of the main land mass.

We had hoped to make use of one of those islands, as a take-off base for the *Polar Star*. Now that they were gone, our next hope lay in the shelter of Drygalski Ice Tongue, as previous expeditions had recorded that close to the promontory was a high plateau. Accordingly, we followed the new ice barrier from longitude 170° 00′ E., heading for longitude 165° 00′ E.; but we found no inlet of any description, and were therefore compelled to skirt the barrier until we came round to the Bay of Whales. Here we encountered an extraordinary sight. The whole bay was frozen, not with ordinary pack ice, but during the process of extension, the ice barrier had thrust out towards the frozen bay with such a force, that the ice which lay within it had crumpled and corrugated, making the whole area resemble the extended bellows of a giant accordion. The outer part which lay next to the open water had the appearance of having been carved out rather like the terracing of a slate quarry. The "step" to which we had sailed close, was eight feet high.

After all our struggles, this seemed to be the last straw. We had faced hazard after hazard without the hope of exploration, let alone the flight of the Polar Star. Our spirits were at such a low ebb that we forgot the date. It was 24th December, which we Norwegians hold as our chief festive day! But after

5 p.m. delicious smells from the galley cheered our hearts. One person had not forgotten, the steward, who was preparing a special evening meal for us. The mess room was so small that we could not celebrate together as one company, and as at every other meal, there had to be three sittings. The first course consisted of stockfish, followed by a joint from our precious supply on the rigging, after which we had tinned fruit and cream. Although fresh fruit was missing, we finished off the meal with beer, champagne, nuts and chocolate. Those replete after the main part of the meal, sat in the corridor drinking beer and champagne, while those still inside the messroom, savoured their meat course. In this way we managed to invoke togetherness and some conviviality.

Mr Ellsworth had declared that we were to consider ourselves on holiday, and as a piece of fun, presented each of us with a toy pocket knife as our Christmas Eve present.

After we had all partaken of the delicious food, our thoughts turned to our respective homes, and while some sat silently with heads bowed gazing at their feet, others regaled the company with stories of Christmas customs in their homelands, sentimental and humorous. When we turned on the radio, from all part of the world came the beloved Austrian Christmas hymn "Heilige Nacht" which we sang to the Norwegian words "Glade jul, Hellige jul", while the Americans sang "Still the Night, Holy the Night". It was a very strange Christmas Eve. Around us lay snow and ice in plenty, but since it was the Antarctic midsummer, it was broad daylight at 11.30 p.m. Instead of having the ideal conditions under which to begin our exploration, 8 sea miles of terraced and corrugated ice lay between us and the Bay of Whales from which we had hoped to make a landing.

As we roved the world by radio, occasionally we heard faint signals in morse interrupting the programmes, but at first we paid little heed to them, thinking that they came from some whaling ship. Later when the tappings became more distinct, the radio officer and I concentrated to try to decode the messages and discovered that they were in an unknown language. Even when we consulted our radio signal station book, we could not find any clue which would have identified the source of the signallings. As the intruding station ceased its tappings just before midnight, we were able to hear joyful bells ring in Christmas from London, New York and Oslo. Then we retired to sleep.

Next morning, after a very satisfying breakfast, I went to the radio room to suggest that we tune in again to find out if the strange station was still on the air. Sure enough, after a few minutes it came through again, very distinctly now, and at more frequent intervals. In fact, each call seemed to get louder. It was no figment of imagination, the source of these morse tappings was close to us, and was coming closer. Yet we were quite unaware of the presence of another ship and certainly from the bridge and even from the "crow's nest" there was no sign of one. Here was a mystery indeed. I went into the wheel-house and spotted Pussy venturing out on the boat deck, the first time since the skirmish with the skuas. She immediately lifted her little nose in the air and began sniffing about in all directions. I thought perhaps she scented the presence of seals, but there were none in sight. Nevertheless, I reckoned that it would be a good idea to follow the clue she was giving by this urgent sniffing, and although it was Christmas Day, I asked if anyone was willing to come ski-ing with me. Three volunteered, one American and two Norwegians.

We prepared the usual equipment necessary for a reconnoitring trip, and with plenty of coffee and special Christmas sandwiches we set out.

Although the step next to the boat was 8 feet high there were several patches where snow had blown against the perpendicular walls, thus providing inclines upon which it was possible for us to ascend. It was exceedingly heavy going to get to the top of each of those steep ascents, and by the time we had come beyond the terraced area, we were out of sight of the ship.

Suddenly, as one man, we pulled ourselves to a standstill, for at our feet were the fresh tracks made by another party of skiers! To the inexperienced, the obvious and only conclusion was that some other people had been there only a short time before, but bending down to examine the marks closely we were able to learn quite a bit about the skiers who had been there so recently. Firstly, the skis were of European manufacture: secondly the men were not only very experienced skiers, but were brilliant, maybe world champions. How did we discern this? From the first traces at our feet, we could see that they knew the trick of the use of seal skin on the underside of the skis, to prevent their sliding backwards on steep inclines. The skins had partly obliterated the sign of the highest grade of skiers, that of the three ridges. But there they were, although the snow powder raised by the skins had brushed over them. Then ahead lay the absolute proof of their prowess, the perfectly straight, parallel, and close lines of the ski tracks, and the regularly spaced marks of the ski sticks. Who had been here just before?

We stopped in cogitation for a moment, as even through our binoculars we could not see anyone at all. Something made me look to the left, and there on the far horizon, a blue haze was rising. I drew the attention of my companions to it, and instead of continuing along the tracks which had been freshly cut, we turned in the direction of the haze. This turned out to be coming from a ship as two masts appeared over the horizon. One mystery solved; here was surely the source of the morse signallings. The reason that we did not know of the ship's whereabouts was that the curved ice barrier had obscured its view from the *Wyatt Earp*. The two ships were lying round the corner from each other, and we had believed ourselves to be alone in the white wilderness.

We had unwittingly taken a short cut when we had turned in the direction of the blue haze instead of pursuing the freshly-cut ski tracks, because very soon we caught up with the party of skiers. There were five of them, who hailed us by clapping their hands. As we did not know their nationality, at first we tried to communicate in English, but in doing so, realized that they knew very few words of it. They, however, solved the problem by switching to very good Swedish. They informed us that they were Russian, and belonged to the ship which we had spotted and suggested that we should return to it with them and meet the rest of their party.

They were dressed in pure white windproof overalls, so the first sight of their return accompanied by us in our bright orange coloured attire must have been a bit of a shock to the men on their ship who were on the look-out for them. As we came within hailing distance, there were great clappings of welcome for us and, when invited to come aboard, we were greeted by the whole ship's company, about forty in all, by cheek to cheek welcomes.

Apparently, although we did not know of the existence of this ship, they knew all about the much publicised *Wyatt Earp* and had expected to meet us. We were first taken to the saloon where we were offered the Russian welcoming drink, vodka. As I had never tasted liquor of any description other than light beer, I confess that I was uneasy about drinking it, and begged to be given a small amount, for I understood that it would be rude to decline it altogether. They smiled and gave me only a small glass, about the size of an egg cup, but even that small quantity made my throat feel as if a red hot poker had been thrust all the way down. The Captain was a charming man and insisted that we stayed to join them for their Christmas lunch. I accepted on behalf of four of us, but asked permission to use their radio to call up the *Wyatt Earp* to explain where we were, and to tell them that the mystery of the unknown signals was solved.

The Christmas meal to which we had been invited was a splendid affair. It was the best meal I had tasted since I left Norway, indeed until the whole expedition was over. The main item on the menu was turkey, and I could hardly believe my eyes when I saw fresh apples and oranges on the table. But a further, greater, surprise was in store. FRESH MILK! This was not reconstituted from an "iron cow" such as we had been presented with from the crew of the *Tafelberg*, but real fresh milk. This puzzled us considerably, until it was explained to us that they had come from Punta Arenas (formerly called Magallanes) in South America, where they had laid in a fresh stock of food and had refilled their deep freeze.

It was astounding to us that they had the means of keeping meat, milk and fruit fresh for an unlimited period. In this, in 1934, the Russians were well ahead. Of course, their ship, a 2,500 tonner, was colossal compared to our little craft. It was similar in type to the British Expeditionary ship *Discovery II*, which was also in the Antarctic at that time. This Russian ship had been built in Murmansk in the north of Russia, and had been constructed for service in polar waters. Although it was a steel ship, it was protected against the ice by oak planks, and had formerly been a fishery patrol boat in the Arctic. Now it was a government expeditionary research ship, fully equipped with a laboratory. We were shown over it, and I was interested to see baskets which were lowered into the water to bring up samples of plankton for study. During the course of conversation, I mentioned having seen minute mosses on the volcanic rocks of Cape Adare, and their scientists informed me that they had samples of them in the laboratory, which they showed me under a powerful microscope.

The ship had just come from the Bellinghausen Sea and was heading in the direction whence we had come. They hoped to visit first Drygalski Island, which had already been claimed by the Russians, and thence to Posadowsky Bay, where they intended to make a landing. From there a party was to head for an area which lay between Princess Elizabeth Land and Wilhelm I Land, to set up a small experimental station.

I was thrilled with the encounter at the time, but now, nearly forty years afterwards, I feel happy to think that I had been privileged to meet these men, for they were the pioneers preparing the way for their fellow countrymen and other scientists to follow.

Without the early mariners, such as Captain Cook, then Rear-Admiral Byrd and this group of Russians, the great onslaught on the Antarctic of 1957 could not have been made. There are now at least seven great Russian stations spread over the Antarctic Continent today, each manned all the year round.

Our ski run back to our own little ship was something which I shall never forget. The time had passed so quickly when we were in the Russian ship that it was late in the evening before any of us realized the time. As it was midsummer day at the South Pole, it was still broad daylight when about 10 p.m. we said "Goodnight and Thank you" to our generous hosts, to set out once more across the frozen bay. That night we saw the south midnight sun as few travellers had ever witnessed it. The display of colours which radiated across the sky, and were reflected on the ice below, produced a phenomenon much too difficult to describe. One usually associates the setting sun with tints of red, but every shade and colour of the solar spectrum filled the air with eerie beauty. It was just on midnight when we reboarded the *Wyatt Earp* and turned to have our last look at the sun as it dipped over the horizon.

The others had not retired to bed as they had awaited our arrival to hear all about the other ship. Mr Ellsworth suggested that in the morning we should call them up to ask if they would be interested to see over our little ship. So after our three sittings of breakfast were over, I went to the radio room to issue the invitation. They assured me that they all would be delighted to take a ski trip over, and would come in relays, to see the little ship which was making headlines in the newspapers of the world.

When they came over, they gasped in disbelief that such a tiny ship could manage to survive the great tortures of the Antarctic, and when they were taken on a tour of inspection, they just could not understand how we could live under such cramped conditions. They all had roomy comfortable cabins, and, for communal use, had a large messroom, saloons, even a cinema and a piano, apart from the laboratory. Our only "Public room", the messroom, could not hold more than six at a time.

We found our new friends to be very congenial and helpful. As they had come from the direction in which we were about to set out, they gave us suggestions about where it might be possible for the *Polar Star* to take off. In fact, not far distant from the position of their ship, they had observed a plateau which could be an ideal take-off spot for the plane. We were extremely glad to learn of this, as we were beginning to think that the whole project would have to be called off.

Mr Ellsworth had been ever optimistic, but Mr Balchen, a very wise and cautious flyer, probably the greatest aviator at that time, had always been against taking unnecessary risks. In Rear-Admiral Byrd's expedition, he had already experienced how unpredictable the weather and ice conditions could be in the region of the South Pole, and even in the best weather how difficult were the flying conditions. However, after meeting those Russians, many of whom were already veteran explorers, he also began to hope for the flight.

It was most interesting to listen to the views of the Russians on the study of the Antarctic. They believed that the mystery of the world lay below that frozen continent, and whichever nation was the first to unravel it, would rule the world. But they added, that if another war should break out, other factors would be revealed so rapidly, that exploration of the Antarctic would no longer be of any consequence.

As I was the only person on the *Wyatt Earp* who could understand the Russian Captain, since the Swedish he spoke was tinged with Finnish, it gave me the opportunity of conversing with him uninterrupted by the others. He asked me if I had read any of the science fiction novels of Jules Verne, who died in 1905, and I told him that I was indeed an ardent admirer of this great French writer, and had read all his books which had been translated into Norwegian, my favourite being *Around the world in Eighty Days*.

When we discussed *De le Terre à la Lune*, the Russian Captain predicted that long before the year 2000, men would attempt to fly to the moon. When I think back to that conversation, I did not realize that at the time the Captain was hinting to me that, even then, the foundations were being laid for exploration beyond the earth's atmosphere. In fact, now I believe that in some way the mission of the scientists who were members of that Russian expedition had been to investigate the possibilities of setting up bases from which outer space could be observed, because the Captain stressed over and over again the vast difference between the rest of the world and the Antarctic, and, for that reason, only from this great frozen South could man, begin to probe into the realms of outer space. I clearly remember our discussion ending with his prognostication that during my lifetime, if not during his own, people would look into a wooden box in their own homes and see men in ships in outer space. As I write this, I wonder if that captain lived to watch the first Russian linking up two space ships and of the American's first moon journey, on his television. I hope he did, for few prophets live to see their prophecies come true.

During the time in which I had been speaking to the Russian Captain, some of the Americans who had not been able to join in any conversation, applied salt to the hatch covers to melt the ice in preparation for taking the *Polar Star* and necessary equipment out of the hold.

The following morning, 27th December, Sir Hubert Wilkins, director of our expedition, decided that he should take a party to inspect the plateau which the Russians had described to us. As Mr Balchen and Mr Ellsworth were to be the heroes of the flight, they accompanied Sir Hubert and along with them they took Liavaag, the A.B./Mate. I was left behind this time to act as host to the Russians who were continuing to come to look over our little ship.

Sir Hubert and his companions returned in the early evening with the information that they had found the plateau exactly as the Russians had depicted it, a great area of newly formed ice projecting for about 4 miles from the barrier. They reckoned that at long last they had found the ideal spot for a take-off base for the *Polar Star*, and had left a ski stick behind, to mark the most suitable place for us to moor the *Wyatt Earp*. The order was then given to start up the engine, and within two hours we reached the mooring place which Sir Hubert had chosen. As soon as the ice anchors were secured, we set to work to unload the equipment and supplies necessary to establish a base.

The Russians gave us invaluable assistance at this stage, as not only had they miniature ice boring drills to gauge the thickness of the ice but they actually had propelled sledges. I had never seen others like them before; the motor turned little paddles at each side of the sledge reminding me of the Mississippi River paddle steamers which I had seen on films. These little sledges could easily travel at a speed of 20 miles per hour, and as they were put at our disposal to drag our own equipment-loaded sledges, they saved us both time and energy; otherwise we would have had to travel by ski and drag our own loads. By using their ice drills, the Russians discovered that next to our ship, the ice was 40 feet thick, but a few miles nearer to the barrier, the thickness of the ice was 60 feet, and it was there that we decided to set up our base.

By New Year's Eve, the base was all ready, and all that remained in preparation was to assemble the *Polar Star* and drag it to its "runway". The skis had already been fitted, but it was still wingless, although it had been taken out from the hold and placed on top of the hatch in readiness for hoisting overboard on to the ice.

The weather was at last propitious. The sun shone brilliantly and we had been free from blizzards for a week. Mr Ellsworth was like a little boy in his excitement, and it infected us all. Even the Russians appeared to share the thrill of anticipation, and as we had been granted a holiday from noon on New

Year's day, the Russians suggested that we should all come to their ship to join them in their New Year's dinner and traditional Russian festivities. As we were tired after our exertions of setting up our base camp, we gladly accepted, knowing, too, that it would be a break and a treat for our steward and mess boy. Someone, however, had to remain on the ship, and it was agreed that the engineer and the A.B. with the broken arm should stay behind.

Our generous Russian friends even provided us with transport so that we would not be tired out by ski-ing, and we had the fun of the "taxi" ride in the little paddle sledges.

We were welcomed aboard with cheers and handclapping, and ushered into their great dining saloon. The main items on the menu at this feast were caviare and salmon, and needless to say there were a number of bottles of vodka on the table. It was a real splendid feast to greet the New Year—1935— but although it was a special occasion, no particular preparations had been made to impress us. As friends, we had been bidden to their board to share their meal.

The language problem produced not only difficulties but a great deal of mirth. The Americans were all monoglot English speakers, while many of the Russians did not understand any English; so it was rather hard work for me to be interpreter to all at one time. During the coffee which followed the meal, our American radio operator was suddenly inspired to impart to our hosts a vital piece of information, namely, that our little Pig, which had been already inspected and admired by the Russians when they came to see over our little ship, could not only grunt, but her talents included sniffing and barking like a dog. The histrionics which followed were no doubt vodka inspired, for he dropped to all fours, and crawled about snorting and sniffing, grunting and barking. The Russians, indeed all of us, were helpless with laughter, but lest anyone believed that he had taken leave of his senses, I explained in Swedish how dear Piggy was to us all, and that to us she was not only a pig, but a pet dog, for most certainly Piggy's voice was at times distinctly canine.

After the coffee session was over, we were treated to a wonderful concert. To our astonishment, the programme included choral music of a standard worthy of any broadcast, as well as a recital of classical piano music. The performance ended with traditional balalaika music and Cossack dances.

But the entertainment was not yet over, for we were shown a beautiful documentary film of Stalingrad, featuring mainly paintings and sculptures as well as some of the more famous buildings. When the film came to an end, we rather reluctantly declared that we ought to return to our little ship, but the Russians insisted that we ended the evening by sampling real Russian tea with lemon. While we drank it, I noticed that nearly all the Russians went out and returned soon afterwards, each man with something in his hand. As we thanked our hosts for the wonderful evening, we were each presented with a parting gift, for the great ship was due to leave its moorings the following morning, and we would not be meeting again. I was given a real bearskin cap, others got mittens, and two were presented with high Cossack boots.

We were escorted back to our own tiny ship on the paddle-sledge taxis. Before bidding our friends goodbye, we arranged to keep in radio contact with each other, and to inform each other of any interesting discovery.

Here there was no feeling of nationalism or competition, we were not American, Russian and Norwegian, but friends and fellow Antarcticans.

1. Rough seas round Cape Horn.

2. The deserted whaling station on Deception Island, with the harbour full of pack ice.

3. *Wyatt Earp* at low water in Deception Island's harbour.

4. The *Polar Star* goes ashore on Deception Island for maintenance.

5. The most southerly graveyard in the world—on Deception Island.

6. *Wyatt Earp* forcing a passage through pack ice.

7. Stuck in the pack ice in the Bay of Whales.

8. Icebergs in Hell's Gate, off the tip of Graham Land.

9. Melting ice at Cape Adare.

o. Penguins on Dundee Island.

1. *Wyatt Earp* moors alongside the ice barriers in the Weddell Sea. Meat is seen hanging in the rigging and the plane floats in the foreground.

12. Men spread out on the ice waiting for rescue after the calving of the barrier.

13. The *Polar Star*, severely damaged when the barrier calved, about to be hoisted aboard *Wyatt Earp*.

14. Nordenskjöld's look-out place above the hut, seen below, built from the wreck of the *Antarctica*. Graham Land mountains in the distance.

15. Stone shelter in which some of Nordenskjöld's men wintered.

16. Taken by the author while flying in *Polar Star* with Sir Hubert Wilkins above the ship entrenched off Dundee Island.

17. (*opposite*) In the Ross Sea, taken from a mound of ice above where the ship lay.

18. The masts and galley chimney of Little America, where the crew of the *Polar Star* waited a month after flying across the Antarctic continent.

19. First to locate the fliers was the British ship *Discovery II*, seen here with the *Wyatt Earp*, showing a relief plane on deck.

CHAPTER FOURTEEN

The Barrier Calves

On the morning of 2nd January, we set to work in earnest in preparation for the flight. The *Polar Star* was hoisted overboard from the hatch, and dragged to the base to be fitted with its wings.

I have so far omitted to mention that we had on board as part of our equipment, a snow tractor which was a small version of the great Sno-cat used by Fuchs and his party on the large-scale 1957 expedition. This was the first time that we had put it into use, and it not only dragged the plane and all the other necessary heavy equipment to the base, but we used it also to prepare the take-off runway.

We were hampered in our task of assembling the plane as we had to work with bare hands on account of the thousands of tiny nuts and bolts required in attaching the wings to the body. Without some kind of heating system, this would have been quite impossible as the temperature was about 25 degrees Centigrade below zero. So we built a canvas enclosure for our workshop, and within its walls we placed four large upright blow-lamps which radiated sufficient heat for us to work without being attacked by frost-bite. As this work of assembling the plane had to be continuous, we worked day and night in four hourly shifts, generally with five men working at a time.

We had to work for two days on the plane before it was ready for a test flight. During the afternoon of 3rd January, we received a radio message from the Russian ship to say that they had encountered snow patches and a strong westerly gale. By this time, their ship had covered a distance of about 400 miles to the west of our position, but as so far everything had gone so well with us we paid little heed to it. However, the blizzard hit us late in the evening of the same day. I was one of those out on the base, and we had our first warning of the approach of the snowstorm from the fact the temperature suddenly rose to about zero.

When the gale was at its height, we had to give up work and retire into the tent for shelter. There, we had all the equipment necessary to make a light meal of hot coffee and sandwiches, and although the blizzard obscured our view of the ship, we remained in contact with it by walkie-talkie radio.

As soon as the storm, which lasted during most of the night, had abated, we emerged to find that everything had been covered up by the drifting snow. Before retiring into the tent for shelter, we had taken the precaution of covering the plane and the fuel drums over with a tarpaulin, to prevent damage, but hours of digging lay ahead before we could come close to the plane to remove its covering. It was fortunate that the snow tractor had not been completely buried, and as soon as it was freed, it was moved some 60 yards away to a place where the snow drifts were not so high, and during the period when three of my companions were feverishly digging away the snow round the plane, the fourth on the snow tractor began to level off a fresh area and so constructed a new runway.

By now the ship had radioed to tell us that reinforcements would arrive to enable the snow clearing operation to be completed as soon as possible, but Sir Hubert Wilkins requested that I return to the ship to join the team comprising Mr Ellsworth, himself, Mr Balchen and the radio operator, in compiling weather charts in preparation for the flight. While I had been up at the base, the radio operator had already received much information from the Russian ship, whaling stations, and ships over a wide area, and from these reports and our own observations, the charts had to be made ready.

By early evening, the charts were ready except for last minute plotting and those up at the base had informed us that all was now ready for flight. They had even heated the engine of the plane. Mr Balchen decided that as the weather conditions were entirely favourable then, he would take up the *Polar Star* for a test flight. I returned to the base with him to see a very different scene from the one which I had left in the morning. A very workable runway had been constructed, and the plane with its engine running was sitting there on its skis like a giant sea bird. I would have welcomed the opportunity to test it myself, it looked so inviting, but of course it was the job and privilege of the senior pilot to do that. As soon as we arrived, Mr Balchen climbed into the cockpit and, with a wave, fixed himself in his seat, pulled over the hatch, set off on the runway and roared up into the air.

We watched with pride and admiration as the great plane encircled the base before heading in a southerly direction. It returned in about an hour's time, and grinning broadly, Mr Balchen jumped down, informing us that the *Polar Star* was in splendid condition; it was to be loaded with fuel and other necessary supplies, and the engine heated up, so that Mr Ellsworth and himself could take off promptly at 9 a.m., the following morning, 5th January.

At long last, the historic flight was to take place, and various sponsors of the expedition had been informed by radio that all was ready. We were glad to retire early, as we had all been working hard during the past four days. Moreover, we could only have a few hours sleep as we had to be up early the following morning to be at the base at 6 a.m. to begin the task of loading the plane and to recheck everything before beginning to heat the engine.

It was a beautiful morning as we skied the four miles to the runway, and it seemed as if everything augured well for the flight.

By 7.30 a.m. unpredicted disaster beset us.

At all times in the Antarctic there are noises, and by this time, we were so accustomed to them we paid little heed to rumbles, until suddenly, from within the deep caverns, far below the surface of the ice barrier, came ominous sounds like the tuning up of a mighty orchestra. It was as if the whole universe itself had begun to vibrate.

For the same reason that during a phenomenon like the total eclipse of the sun, when birds and beasts are numbed into silence, this unexpected, demoniac, and mighty stridulation, paralysed us into total immobility. We stood rooted to the spot, so great was the terror which engulfed us. As the ominous sound continued, it was as if a mammoth organ, hidden behind macrocephalic stalactites, began to play accompanied by gigantic "cymbal" crashes.

Although I could neither move nor turn my eyes to see the reaction of my companions, I experienced the strange sense of my brain beginning to function again after the first petrifying attack of paralysis, and I tried to combat the terror I still experienced by likening each new sound to another orchestral instrument. A sudden shrill whistling noise, I told myself, was the piccolo, and percussive twangings, like the clinking of millions of pendants hanging from colossal chandeliers, could be translated into the performance of a 100 pianos and millions of castanets. I began to imagine that I was standing all alone, surrounded by thousands of xylophones and glockenspiels. Then involuntarily my eyes moved and, in the distance, I saw the masts of our little ship, dancing to the rhythm of the unending and thunderous *ostinato*.

This jolted me into reality, and the noise of the "concert" was temporarily blotted out, as I began to reason why the ship should be moving. New faint sounds could now be heard during the brief pause in the pulsating hollow bass. This was no imagination; it was the sound of splashing water, explaining without doubt, the movement of the ship. Our base was no longer a plateau, but a series of ice floes which had begun to drift from each other.

Before those terrifying blastings and crashings had subsided, I discovered that I was alone on an ice-floe! Beside me was a cluster of oil drums which rolled backwards and forwards as the ice raft rocked violently. I looked in the direction where the plane had sat waiting to take off, but there was no sign of it, and only one of the mechanics stood on an ice floe which had been part of the runway.

Little did we dream that morning of 5th January 1935, that we would be—perhaps the closest witnesses of all time—right on the spot when the barrier decided to calve. How we escaped with our lives is nothing short of a miracle. The noises which had terrified us so much were the cracking, ripping and breaking, of miles of thickly packed ice which may have taken as many as 1,000 years to form.

During the previous year on the rare occasions when it had been possible to make a landing on the barrier, we had come close to giant rifts in the ice, so deep that it was impossible for the eye to estimate the depth. Kneeling as close to the edge of them as safety allowed, one saw first of all that the colour appeared to be green merging into a hazy blue through which no human sight could penetrate. On one occasion I dropped an empty oil barrel into one of those mighty crevasses, and judging by the time it took for sound of its descent to fade away, we estimated that the depth was over 1,000 feet. The farthest downwards the eye can see is about 100 feet.

Therefore when the barrier calves, it splits at those crevasses and thereby the first range of icebergs are formed. When these part from the parent ice, they are thrust out with such a force that the ice on the frozen creeks crumples and breaks.

This thrusting outwards of the newly formed icebergs had not only cracked our plateau but, having divided it, the floes and bergs were at once scattered over a wide area.

As there had been nine of us working with the plane, I wondered what had happened to the other seven. The ship had not been destroyed, although it had been pushed much further away by the force of the ice-quake. As we always carry whistles when we leave the ship, I blew mine, and after a few seconds came answering blasts from all directions, although I could not see my companions as the newly-formed icebergs obscured the view. Assured that some were still alive, I turned to see the new barrier. It was as if a wave of a wand had changed the entire scenery. A little more than an hour before, it had been a scene of great ethereal beauty, with its millions of stalactites of all sizes hanging from it. Now it looked as if a great invisible slicer had been at work, removing all the ragged edges, for there the new barrier stood, a shining straight wall, like a tower of finely chiselled crystal.

It was bitterly cold, and I do not think that I had ever felt so lonely before. After I had blown my whistle, the answer- ings sounds suggested that some of the others were together behind a towering berg, but the only human I could see was the mechanic who kept floating away from me.

The *Wyatt Earp* at this point was only a speck in the distance, and I noticed that she had begun to move, but not in my direction. Was my only hope of being rescued disappearing for ever? As I stood watching her go out of sight, it began to snow fairly heavily, but not a blizzard by Antarctic standards, as I could still see a glow of light through it.

About half an hour later, the snow cleared slightly, enabling me to catch a glimpse of the ship reappearing as she zigzagged her way through the ice floes. But my glimpse of her was only momentary as she disappeared altogether again behind a giant iceberg. It seemed an eternity as I stood alone with the oil drums, a piece of canvas, and some planks. I could if necessary, have rigged up some kind of shelter, but without food I would not have survived for long. I did not panic, but I knew that I had to keep up my circulation and body heat, so I walked round and round my ice floe like a poor lonely goldfish in a bowl.

A few hours later, my spirits rose as the bow of the *Wyatt Earp* reappeared from the other side of the giant iceberg which had obscured her from me for so long. But had I been spotted, or given up as lost? I had not long to wait, because a few minutes after the ship came into full view, I spotted a dinghy coming towards me with two men in it. When they reached me—about mid-day—they gave me some sandwiches which the steward had prepared, and a thermos flask of hot coffee. Although I was unable to eat, I gladly drank the coffee. Our meeting was very unemotional and matter of fact; there was no time for conversation, for as soon as I had swallowed the coffee, they told me that we had to hurry back in order to try to save the *Polar Star*.

We had a very great struggle to reach the place where my companions believed the *Polar Star* to be, because we could only paddle a short distance at a time between one ice floe and another, dragging the dinghy over the ice until we reached water again.

It took us about an hour to reach the nearest giant iceberg, which had thrust forward between the spot where I had been marooned, and the former runway, breaking up the base as it had forced its way into the water.

An extraordinary sight met our eyes as we approached the other side of this giant obstacle. There was the plane, its body partly submerged between two ice floes upon which its wings rested, and which had prevented it—so far—from sinking entirely. On each of the two floes stood groups of men beside part of the equipment which had escaped damage.

The movement of ice had formed a small lagoon, the great

iceberg supporting the floes at each side of it, and so preventing their drifting apart.

Had there been an opportunity to take a photograph, I could have captured the greatest freak picture of the year, but even if a camera had been available, there would not have been a moment to spare, so great was the urgency to try to save the plane.

Fortunately the great thrusting movement of the berg had sent some of the ice upwards, and we took advantage of those newly-formed ice pillars as mooring uprights, for supporting the plane. There were still wires and ropes lying around, and we set to work immediately to attach them to the plane for temporary mooring, until the ship could approach and hoist the *Polar Star* on board.

The *Wyatt Earp* in her turn had been having its own troubles, and although she was well within our view, it took some considerable time before she could come close enough to be of any assistance. At a distance of 80 yards from the plane, the ship was compelled to stop, but the derrick had been swung over in readiness with wires laid out from the windlass. It now depended on those of us on the floes to secure the plane to the wires. As the ship had moored alongside one of the ice floes upon which rested a wing of the plane, it was not difficult to reach it and drag the wires over to the body. Once attached, the supporting wires had to be made as taut as possible to enable the plane's engine and electrical equipment to be kept above the water. When all was ready, the ship began to move very slowly and carefully round the floe to the mouth of the lagoon, in preparation for the difficult task of hoisting the plane on board.

So far, it appeared as if the plane was intact, but it was impossible to assess likely damage to the undercarriage or landing gear. Therefore, as soon as the *Polar Star* had been secured by mooring it to the ice pillars, every man at once set about doing his best to try to save as much as possible of the plane and its equipment. The propeller was detached and moved to safety, then a group took turns of crawling over the wings, to bring out the equipment which had been stowed inside the plane immediately before the elements had gone beserk.

It had been no easy job to manœuvre the ship into position for the plane dragging and hoisting operation to begin, but our very able seamen succeeded in bridging the lagoon, with the forepart of the *Wyatt Earp* alongside one of the reef floes, while the stern was moored to the other.

In order to prevent ice damage to the wings while the plane was being dragged towards the ship, we had padded each wing with canvas, then we levered one at a time on to skids which we had constructed by nailing together boards and planks brought from the ship, and from wood which was still lying about on the floes. Then the operation of dragging the plane began. But so much care had to be exercised, that the movement was almost imperceptibly slow. We helped the plane on its way, each one crossing our fingers mentally in the hope that by some miracle it was totally undamaged, and that a flight could still be attempted from another plateau or island.

As there was no time for anyone to stop for a meal, the steward and mess boy did their share by going the rounds with hot coffee and sandwiches to keep us warm and to prevent our energy from flagging. We were very grateful for their attention, for it took many hours to drag the *Polar Star*, inch by inch, until it was close enough to the ship for the derricks to hoist it aboard. I think that by that time all our hearts were racing, not only from exertion, but in anticipation of the moment when the undercarriage of the plane would be revealed; and only then would we know for certain if the flight could still be attempted.

There was a deathly silence as the plane was lifted up. Then we saw the havoc that the elements had wreaked upon the *Polar Star*. The guards protecting the hydraulic system had been completely stove in, and the landing gear bent backwards. Much repair would have to be done before the plane could ever be made safe for any flight, let alone such an adventurous one as crossing the Antarctic continent.

We were all now like mourners assembled at a graveside. There was hardly one member of the expedition without tears in his eyes, and several wept openly. To think of all the storms that our little ship had weathered, and the many perils and frustrations that we had endured since we had left Bergen in August 1933 in order to make this flight possible; having come so close to achieving it, the evil genius of the frozen South, had snatched the opportunity from within our grasp.

CHAPTER FIFTEEN

Icebound again

It was therefore with a great feeling of defeat that we watched the wreck of the *Polar Star* being hoisted aloft by the derricks to be placed on top of the hatch. We clambered aboard and assisted in its being secured with wires, but we had as much heart in this task as a person who had lost a loved one and is preparing for the funeral. The job completed we wandered aimlessly about, dead tired, and not knowing what to do.

I think that it was after 11 p.m. when delicious smells from the galley put an end to our brooding. Although it was nearly twenty hours since last we had a real meal, no one actually experienced hunger; all we wanted was rest and sleep, so great was our fatigue, yet our minds were still too numb to think about going to bed. Our good friend the steward understood us perhaps better than we ourselves did, for he had made sure that this particular meal would consist of ingredients from which such appetizing smells would emanate that at least our mouths would salivate and our thoughts return to normal— and messroom-wards! I do not know what we would have done without this steward. We had nicknamed him "the Weather Man" during our first journey through the Roaring Forties, but we were to learn that his culinary art was to inspire us many times in difficulty. On this occasion, he proved to be a psychiatrist. While we had stood about in a dejected state he had gone into action, and it was not long before the first sitting of six men were summoned to partake of the meal.

Our stomachs replete, we began to feel relaxed and drowsy, as one by one we retired to our respective cabins. Although I was glad to flop on to my bunk, it was a long time before sleep overtook me. The extraordinary events of the day rolled round and round in my head. Not one man had spoken during the meal, therefore the subject of the catastrophe had not been introduced. I therefore lay trying to figure out the series of events which had ended in the destruction of the plane. I could still hear those terrible noises which preceded the calving of the barrier, weird unearthly sounds which I could not obliterate from my mind. Even the music composed later by Vaughan Williams for the film *Scott of the Antarctic* was like nursery music compared to these terrorizing sounds which still haunted me.

At length, I dropped off to sleep and the next thing I knew was the mess boy wakening me with the message from Sir Hubert Wilkins that as there was a fierce blizzard raging outside, work of further salvage work was impossible that day, and if I did not want to get up, I could lie in bed. However, I had the resilience of youth, and refreshed I rose and dressed myself. When I reached the messroom the first breakfast sitting was in progress, so I went along to the galley to join the steward in a cup of coffee. I had hoped that he would have told me the version of the upheaval as seen from the ship, but he was strangely silent. I was glad therefore that as soon as I had drunk my coffee, there was a place for me in the messroom. My appetite had returned, and I was glad of the opportunity of having a leisurely meal during which I expected that my companions would be willing to tell me their stories. But no one wished to talk at all.

After everyone had eaten, Sir Hubert Wilkins gathered us together in a corridor, and told us that we were not to break our hearts over "that thing on deck with the broken legs". He added that there was no hurry to leave the area, even if the weather had made it possible; therefore Mr Ellsworth and he had decided that from then on we would change the purpose of the expedition from that of the flight to one of exploration. Much had still to be discovered for the benefit of posterity, and if we could make any contribution, our efforts would not have been in vain. "So," he added, "let us say 'Skol' to that, and drink to our success in champagne." The mess boy was quick to act on his cue word, and suddenly appeared on the scene with bottles of champagne and enough glasses, cups and beakers to go round; this enabled everyone, including himself, to clink receptacles to our future luck, look each other in the eye, and say "skol"!

When the "skolling" was over, and we were sipping our champagne with relish, Sir Hubert informed us that our present imprisonment was not serious, as we could remain here without inconvenience for a further fortnight if necessary and ended with the words "So, boys, enjoy your summer holidays!"

Sir Hubert's own calm and indomitable spirit had saved the situation. Outside, the weather was so bad that it was quite impossible to make any attempt at retrieving our abandoned equipment, but his whole attitude to everything had so cheered us that along with the afterglow of the champagne, we were at last impelled to tell our versions of the great drama which had been enacted on the previous day.

First came the scene as viewed from the ship. Breakfast was still in progress, although some of the men who had already eaten were relaxing in the corridor, when without warning came thunderous noises like the volleys of countless mighty guns and rifles, plus the exploding of thousands of tons of dynamite. They had been startled and numbed by the noise coming through the air, but the sound had sent vibrations, originating in the water beneath the vast protrusion formed by the stalactites on the barrier, to travel beneath our plateau, until they reached the ship, to hit its sides with a curious mixture of rappings and cracklings. Then it seemed as if a tidal wave had struck them, for suddenly all the dishes were swept from the messroom table, the pots and pans from the galley stove, and drawers and every movable object hurled from its position in the cabins. The men on board each grabbed the nearest fixture to him, and hung on for dear life as the ship rocked and rolled quite out of control. Furthermore, with each violent movement of the boat, it hit the ice, and each man had feared that its sharp edge would reduce the little *Wyatt Earp* to matchwood.

The violent tossing and pounding ceased as suddenly as it had begun. As soon as it was possible to do so each man had grabbed his binoculars and rushed to a vantage point to find the cause of the turbulence and discover what had happened to us, out there on the ice.

With great relief they had counted nine, which meant no life had been lost.

When they had located the plane, they were mystified; it

appeared to be intact except for the fact that it was without its legs, and was resting on its body. While all binoculars had been directed towards the plane, Mr Ellsworth had called out, "Never mind about the plane, that does not worry me, but get out and rescue those boys before anything else happens."

However, before rescue operations could be put into action, they had prepared a chart, plotting the position of each one of us, stranded on the ice, lest a blizzard should blow up, preventing their reaching us. This task, which had stirred them into action, had obviated the numbness of their brains, brought on by the sudden cataclysm. Our positions plotted, a brief discussion had been held about the best way to manœuvre the ship, so that she could be brought as close as possible to us to simplify the rescue work.

While I listened to this account, I sat quietly in a corner with Pussy in my arms, stroking her gently, and wondering even then if everything had really happened, or had I imagined the whole thing. There was a short pause for discussion and a smoke before the others, who had been on the ice, told their story; I slipped away with Pussy in my arms in search of dear little Piggy to find out how things were with her. I think it was then, alone in the company of the two little animals, that I really came to myself, and felt glad to be alive. But the question which remained uppermost in my mind was, "Would the dangers of the Antarctic ever be overcome?"

For reasons which I could not explain, tears came into my eyes, as Pussy, purring contentedly within my anorak, and Piggy nuzzling up against my thigh snortled happily. Occasionally, she glanced up in Pussy's direction, and gave an extra grunt if the cat closed her eyes, lest Pussy should fall asleep. These two little animals appeared to have a great sense of understanding between them, and I felt, together, they were trying to ease my tension.

I do not know how long I had been together with my little friends, when suddenly the small dynamo motor started up. This startled me out of my reverie, and I returned to join the others and find out why the dynamo was in action. It had been started by the radio operator on the instruction of Mr Ellsworth, so that a message could be put through to the *New York Times*—one of the sponsors of the expedition—to inform them that the flight had to be abandoned because of the broken plane.

In spite of Sir Hubert's encouragement, there was still an atmosphere of anticlimax hanging over us. When I returned to the conference corridor, after my interlude with the animals, the story as experienced by those of us on the ice plateau, had already been told. I was glad to have been spared my share in telling, for I just wanted to relax and forget about it for the time being. The others seemed as if once they had been gathered together, they could not part from each other. I wished I could have advised them to do as I had done in seeking out the animals; but, somehow, I could not bring myself to give the advice. As usual, it was the steward and the mess boy who rose to the occasion by announcing that the coffee kettle would be kept hot in the galley and we could help ourselves at any time. This invitation was timely, for I feared that our *esprit de corps* would literally cramp us to the point when the continual sight of each other's faces in that tiny corridor would eventually drive us crazy.

There was a diversion when the Russian ship came through on the radio, to ask how things were with us, as we had been out of contact for some time. When told what had happened, they immediately offered to turn back and come to our assistance. However, we assured them that we were all right, although we thanked them gratefully for their offer of help.

The gales and blizzards continued to keep us prisoners for another five days, but there was a temporary lull in the storm on 12th January which enabled us to leave the ship in relays to try to recover the equipment which lay abandoned on the ice floes. At first it seemed as if the plateau had been reformed, as the blown snow had bridged over many of the gaps between the floes. It was still bitterly cold, but we were glad to feel the freedom again as we went in search of the lighter pieces of equipment which we dragged back on the sledges. The tractor still stood where it had been left when it had completed the runway, and after removing snow which surrounded it, we put it into action to bring back the heavy oil and petrol drums. It was driven to within 25 yards of the ship where ropes were attached to the drums which were swung aboard by the derricks. We had to give up work for the night before getting the tractor aboard because of the intense cold.

Overnight another blizzard raged, and when we looked out in the morning, we could not understand why the tractor looked so strange. It was at an extraordinary angle, and only the back part of one of the caterpillar tracks was visible. At once most of us went overboard to dig away the snow and get it into a position for loading, but just as we approached it sank out of sight. One of the mechanics had actually reached it, and I took a photo of him as he knelt at the edge of the floe and watched it drop into the water below.

It was aggravating to lose this valuable piece of equipment so near to bringing it aboard, but by now we had learned our lesson to guard against despondency; so we took this loss philosophically, and returned to the ship to wait until the weather permitted us to move on to a more favourable mooring place where some exploration might be possible.

CHAPTER SIXTEEN

Dynamite for Freedom

By 15th January the gales had subsided, but owing to the continuous blizzards of the past few days, the cracks between the floes had filled up with snow which had frozen over; once more the ship was stuck fast in the ice.

Although it was still bitterly cold, the sun was shining brilliantly as we finished our breakfast that day. In spite of Sir Hubert's assurance that we had plenty of time to linger here until the ice broke up, the brighter weather and anticipation of exploration gave us all the urge to get away from that place. As our only engine was not sufficiently powerful, I asked Sir Hubert if we might try to force a channel to the open water by using the dynamite which we had bought in New Zealand. He told me that he had already been considering that possibility, and agreed to give the order to begin drilling holes into which sticks of dynamite could be placed.

We had on board two drills, but not so sophisticated as the motor-driven ones used by the Russians. Ours had to be operated by hand, and could only reach a depth of about 10 feet at the most. Each consisted of a steel bar, at the end of which were attached two spoonlike projections which revolved to scoop away the ice as we turned the handle at the top of the bar.

The first hole, roughly 6 feet deep, was drilled about 10 yards away from the ship. In it we placed a long bamboo cane to which were bound five sticks of dynamite, one on top of the other, with the detonating caps upwards. To each of the caps was attached a wire leading to the electric firing battery. When the detonators were fired, the result was no more spectacular than if someone had lit a match on which the flame had extinguished itself as soon as the head had been struck.

We then moved further away from the ship to between 35 and 40 yards. Here we drilled two holes, each of which was 8 feet deep. In one of them the drill went right through the ice, and water began to seep upwards. In each hole were placed as many sticks of dynamite as the bamboo cane could hold, but in the hole through which the drill had penetrated as far as the water, the dynamite was lowered so that the explosion would take place below the ice. The sticks were detonated simultaneously, but the only one which had much effect was that which had been exploded in the water; this threw up the ice recently formed over the previous gaps between the floes, and once again the giant cracks were revealed.

The partial success gave us the idea of resuming the drilling, not from the ship outwards towards the open water, but from the new and thinner ice which lay next to it. Here we had much more success, and by taking the drilling in turns, I think that in all we bored over a hundred holes, through which we blasted sufficient dynamite to cut a channel out into open water.

As the stern frame and the rudder were completely encased in a large ice lump, it was quite out of the question to start the engine, for in doing so the cracking of the shaft and damage to the blades of the propeller were inevitable. But we had to come well out into open water before we could take any measures to free the ship of the ice which also stuck fast to the sides. We had no alternative but to drag our little ship through the newly-formed channel by means of the ice anchors; these were attached by ropes to the windlass and the ship was then pulled forward into open water. With the rudder in a fixed position because of the encasement in the ice, we could not steer the ship in the orthodox fashion by means of the wheel, so we hoisted the fore and aft sails, which responded to the light south-westerly breeze, by allowing us to manœuvre the ship as well as giving us movement.

Once clear of the 8 foot new frozen ledge surrounding the old ice floes, we had to attempt to thaw some of the ice which was still clinging to the ship and impeding our progress. The water itself was not sufficiently salty, so we had to take other measures, well known to the members of the expedition who had already had much experience in the frozen waters of the

Arctic. On board, we had stacked, together with the fuel barrels, a few drums containing lumps of carbide. We made several small packages of the coke-like lumps in thick paper bags, and placed them in four jute sacks containing rock salt. Two of the jute bags were then slung over each side of the stern of the ship, and when the water seeped through to the paper bags containing the carbide, heat was generated; together with the action of the salt this heat burnt its way into the hard ice until it disintegrated and fell off.

After a few hours, the mixture of salt and carbide had melted the ice surrounding the rudder, and it could again move freely. This enabled us to steer the ship in the orthodox manner, although we did not yet dare use the engine. There was a light following breeze, and after hoisting the main sail, we were able to proceed at a leisurely speed of 2 knots, with our course set for King Edward VII Land, before heading out into the Roald Amundsen Sea.

On 18th January, Sir Hubert Wilkins called us together for a conference. He was a wonderful leader, and never made decisions without giving us the opportunity either of making suggestions, or of declining to undertake tasks if we felt unable to carry them out. But I think that most of us trusted Sir Hubert so implicitly that we gladly followed his ideas. Accordingly, when he told us of the plan which had been formulating in his mind, we listened eagerly.

He explained that, since the flight had not taken place, we were carrying far too much fuel aboard, and that we should have to get rid of it if we were to linger in the Antarctic in order to carry out any exploration. After conferring with Mr Ellsworth and by radio with our sponsors in America, he informed us that it had been decided that the ship would spend the Antarctic winter in South America, possibly in Montevideo or Buenos Aires, while the plane was returned to U.S.A. for repair. A flight would be attempted again the following year, taking off possibly somewhere near Palmer Land.

Accordingly, he had thought of the possibility of our setting up three bases between Little America and Graham Land, in case the *Polar Star* should have to land, short of fuel, during its flight. This would not only rid us of our unwanted cargo, but give us invaluable experience in the setting up of bases, which at that time was still an innovation in the Antarctic. Sir Hubert warned us, however, that it would be very hard going, since we had lost our snow tractor, and we would have to drag the heavy barrels on sledges, perhaps for many miles, using skis or snow shoes. He added that under those conditions he could not compel any of us to take part if we were not inclined to do so, therefore he—with his eyes fixed on ME—called for volunteers. I responded with a wink, and as I watched him look round the company, I wondered how many of my companions had simultaneously made up their minds to take part in this new venture. He told us that he himself would lead the party, and my joy knew no bounds at the prospect of following this great man on the barrier. His eyes returned to meet mine, and he visibly grinned. He rarely laughed, but when he smiled his little beard suddenly shot outwards, and then we were assured of his approval. I did not care if I had been the only volunteer, I looked up to Sir Hubert as a dog does to his master. It was a tremendous honour to serve under such a great explorer.

After there had been a general assent to the project, although the number of volunteers was still unknown, Sir Hubert told us that should we meet any whaling boats, we would request to purchase from them fresh meat, potatoes and vegetables, adding with another twinkle in his eye, that nothing deters a good explorer more than an unvaried diet of tinned food.

Sir Hubert, anxious that we were absolutely sure of our own minds before committing ourselves in front of each other, suggested that while we thought the matter over, we should have a hot cup of coffee. As we took our places on the floor of our conference room—the narrow corridor—he went to his cabin and returned with an unopened bottle of *Marie Brizard*, which he shared with all of us. As no liqueur glasses are generally available on an Antarctic expedition, we savoured the delectable flavour mixed with the coffee.

Most of us volunteered to go when finally the show of hands was asked for, but Sir Hubert, tactful to the extreme, said that while he would not stop anyone from coming, some had to remain to look after the ship, and the more powerful men were necessary to take turns of dragging the sledges with the equipment. In this way no one was made to feel less important than the others, but it was obvious that he was anxious that those like myself who were natural skiers, should choose to go all the way with him.

The men who had to remain behind were the Captain, the radio officer, the doctor, the steward, the chief engineer, and the A.B. who had the broken arm. By this time the Captain, a very able and experienced Arctic navigator, was suffering from heart trouble due to the rigours enforced upon us during the fortnight when we were entrenched in the ice, and had to remain inside. While he was always available to give advice, between us we had relieved him of all bridge duty during the past few weeks, and the doctor's skill kept him going until we reached South America.

In order to emphasize the importance of the men who would volunteer to take it in turn to do the shorter ski runs and drag the equipment in turns, Mr Ellsworth and Mr Balchen declared that they would remain based on the ship, and see to the loading of the sledges as well as taking spells of the shorter ski runs.

The mess boy was an expert skier, and the steward, whom I suspect would like to have taken the trip himself, offered to do the menial tasks such as dish washing, to free the mess boy for the landing party. The other volunteers consisted of the second and third engineers, both the mechanics, Liavaag, and myself.

Satisfied with our response, Sir Hubert Wilkins laid his plans before us. The first consideration, he pointed out, was to select the mooring shelters for the *Wyatt Earp*. As he was addressing us, the ship still had her course set for King Edward VII Land, but soon we would be rounding the point into Biscoe Bay. Sir Hubert informed us that in order to proceed with the project the first base should be set up as soon as possible, and therefore he was considering Block Bay—a tiny inlet which lies east of Sulzberger Bay—as our mooring place while we set up our first base.

Holding a detailed map of the coastline against a wall, Sir Hubert then pointed out to us the other sheltering inlets which we could use later on. If the setting up of the first base proved to be successful, we would follow the coastline in the Amundsen Sea until we came to Bear Island, where there was a suitable little cove for the ship to lie while the second base was established. Then moving his pencil until he came to Alexander I

Island, he pointed to a creek on the landward side called Ronne Bay. This, he declared would be the ideal base for the ship while the landing party explored the mainland for a suitable site for base No. 3. Then, as an afterthought, he added that should we achieve our aim of setting up the three bases as planned, we could even attempt to set up a fourth if the Antarctic winter did not descend upon us too soon. Thus, if the weather and ice conditions favoured us, we could moor the ship off Adelaide Island, which lies off Graham Land, and set up our fourth base in that area. Failing that, we could sail around Snow Hill Island and Dundee Island before setting course for Montevideo to tie up the ship for the winter months.

Having outlined his plans for the potential ship positions, he then told us briefly of the requirements of each base, and listed the following essential items which we would leave in readiness for the following year.

(1) 6 drums of plane fuel.
(2) 1 drum of oil.
(3) 1 10 gallon drum of kerosene.
(4) 1 steel spade.
(5) 1 wooden spade.
(6) 1 broom.
(7) 1 canvas, plus ropes to secure it.
(8) 1 large bamboo pole, with orange flags to mark the spot after it had been covered with snow, and lastly,
(9) tins of food.

After that, Sir Hubert explained the procedure for the construction of the first base. Everyone not required to remain on the ship would set out together and ski for four hours, taking it in turns to drag the heavy sledges. Then we would stop for a meal and a rest. The food would be previously prepared on board and placed in a container, so that it would only require to be reheated at the first stop. After that the party would then divide, and the group to return to the ship would be Mr Ellsworth, Mr Balchen, the two mechanics and the second engineer. Sir Hubert, Liavaag, the mess boy, the third engineer and myself would continue with the equipment. The five of us would take a second break, pitching a tent for a night, and then continue until we came to a point 77° 00′ S. and 13° 15′ W.

That made a distance from the ship of 100 kilometres, and there he hoped that conditions would favour us to establish the base.

Now that the plans had been fully explained to us, Sir Hubert took us to the hold where the clothing and equipment were stacked. Since we left New Zealand there had been no facilities for washing our clothes, and he decided that the time had now arrived when a new issue was necessary. We were each supplied therefore with a complete new outfit, from the layer next to our skin out to the thick Icelandic jersey which we normally wore below our anoraks. We were even given the option of having new ski boots, but we all declined as we preferred to hang on to those which had already moulded to the shape of our feet rather than be plagued by blisters inflicted by stiff new leather. The five of us, including Sir Hubert himself, who were to tackle the longer journeys in order to set up the bases, would each be supplied with a double outfit, so that we could take spares along with us.

While we were in the hold we checked the sledges to see if they were in perfect order; although no damage had been done, we fitted one of them with wider runners.

Until that time we had been depending entirely on our sails to get along, but Sir Hubert gave the order to the engineers to try to turn the engine by hand, using steel bars to ascertain whether or not the propeller was yet free of ice before it was safe to give the order "Full steam ahead". With great glee, the engineers informed us that at last the propeller was free.

We felt that we had been given a new lease of life as once again the engine throbbed into action; we were eager for the next phase of our adventure to begin, as we sighted the great volcanic rocks which shelter the lagoon towards which we were heading. It was in the early evening of 19th January that we sailed into Block Bay, which we found to our amazement was almost entirely free of ice.

Our greatest surprise was not the discovery that there was very little ice in the inlet, but that on the rocks was the largest colony of penguins which we had encountered so far. As one bird, millions of them rushed forward to give us a royal welcome. So great was their excitement and urge to get the best possible vantage point that when we went overboard to secure the ice anchors, they positively impeded our efforts to moor the ship.

Everything had to be inspected by them with sniffing and beak tapping; we could not move through them because of their inspection of our legs. As they obscured the anchor ropes by standing on them, we were compelled to move the birds aside with a broom handle until the ship was at last securely moored to the ice ledge. The birds were not in any way scared or offended by our pushing them aside, for once the anchors were in position they closed their ranks again, quacking so loudly that we had to bellow to each other in order to be heard above the din of the birds.

As usual, after the ship had been moored, we put out the gangway and went along to the corridors to enjoy a cup of hot coffee. We had hardly begun to sip the steaming liquid when loud laughter came from the galley and the steward called out —"We have visitors, boys." We hurried on deck to see what it was all about, and discovered the gangway crammed with penguins marching on board. Already about twenty of them were strutting about the deck, no doubt feeling that they were returning the compliment which we had paid to them by visiting their territory and assuming that the gangway had been placed for them. Although they presented a very funny spectacle, and I for one would love to have allowed them to stay, we were compelled to drive our visitors back the way they came, and pull back the gangway for fear that the whole colony would swarm aboard the ship. The birds which were already on deck were dropped overboard on to the ice quacking resentfully.

After the evening meal was over, this was the first time since leaving New Zealand in October that we could retire to bed, fully relaxed, knowing that the ship was securely anchored in a safe mooring place, sheltered by solid rocks.

CHAPTER SEVENTEEN

First Base set up

Next morning, 20th January, I awakened feeling very refreshed after a good night's sleep. The first sound I heard was not the usual call by the mess boy, but the voices of the thousands of penguins as they thronged forward to get a glimpse of the activity on board.

The steward had been up and about early collecting penguins' eggs for our breakfast, and by the time I reached the galley the morning coffee was already in progress amidst much mirth and laughter as each one vied with the others in mimicry of the penguins which looked like a mass meeting of waiters.

I should stress that penguin eggs are never boiled, poached, or fried, as although the yolks make delicious omelettes and are very good for baking purposes, the white savours too much of cod liver oil to be palatable.

It was a beautiful clear morning with brilliant sunshine, although the slight breeze was bitingly cold. Nevertheless, we were excited to get on with our preparations for setting out the following day on our long ski run. As soon as everyone had partaken of penguin omelette we separated into groups to divide the work of preparation so as to have everything ready for setting off the following morning at 8 a.m.

First of all the damaged plane had to be dismantled and restacked in its hold for safety. Therefore, while one group was at work removing the wings and tail of the plane, the rest of us began to assemble the equipment which was to be dragged to the base. Sir Hubert and I attended to the packing of the delicate instruments of navigation which we were to take with us. Before doing so, however, it was necessary to correct any deviation on the two compasses which we were to take with us. To do this I had to leave the ship with one of them while Sir

Hubert went to the wheel-house with the other; from our respective positions, we each took bearings to find out possible deviations, as sometimes the engine or steel fittings of a ship can result in slight alterations on a compass. After this was done and the other instruments checked, we stacked them in a long wooden case, ready to be placed on one of the sledges.

After lunch, we all assisted in the lowering into the hold of the body of the *Polar Star*, and securing it into position for the rest of the journey. This kept us busy until 3.30 p.m., coffee time, after which we turned to sledge loading. All was ready by the time we had our evening meal, and we retired to our bunks, ready for sleep, but in eager anticipation of the morrow.

Breakfast had to be over by 6.30 a.m. the following morning, so we were awakened at 4 a.m., for the first sitting to begin at 5 a.m. An issue to each man of two bucketfuls of tepid water gave us the unaccustomed luxury of a good wash down, and we began the day feeling that life was really worth living.

The landing party set off at 8 a.m. in brilliant sunshine, dragging three sledges. The way was slow going at the beginning, as we had to make a detour round the penguin camp to get clear of the birds; but in spite of our efforts, thousands of them followed us. Our speed was much too swift for their shuffling steps, so they flopped on to their stomachs, using their feet as propellers and their flippers to balance themselves, as they pursued us over the rough ice.

Sir Hubert was happy that the penguins had attached themselves to us, explaining that if a penguin went ahead of one, it was safe to follow it, as they sensed the cracks in the ice on the barrier, and always avoided them.

So far we had no need of the compasses as we had the mountains ahead as landmarks, with the dark sky, a sure sign of open water, behind us and above the ship. After about two or three hours we reached the top of the incline and were on a level plateau. Most of the birds had retreated to their colony, but we still had a few stragglers in pursuit; soon these realized that our goal was further away than they wished to travel, and they too returned to their homes.

At mid-day we approached some volcanic rocks where we found both shelter and warmth, so stopped for coffee and sandwiches. After our light repast we wandered over the rocks, and only 20 yards from where we had been sitting, the heat from the rocks, combined with the brilliant sun, compelled us to take off our anoraks. Some of the party would like to have removed more of their clothing to sunbathe, but there was no time for loitering.

Refreshed, we continued on our way in a south-easterly direction. About 2 p.m. a mountain top completely devoid of ice and snow came into sight, but before heading towards it we took a last glance at the barrier below us, which from our vantage point appeared to be quite flat. The ship was still in sight, a mere speck, and above it, reflecting the open water, was the dark navy-blue sky. We stopped to have our mid-day meal of *lobscouse*, a hash made from potatoes, meat and vegetables. This spot, Sir Hubert decided, would be the parting of the ways; it was the place where we should leave one of the heavy sledges, which we of the advance party should pick up the following day, after we had gone ahead and set up the base. At 4 p.m. the men who were to return to the ship left us, and we reckoned that travelling light it would take them roughly three and a half or four hours to make the ski run back to the ship. We watched them head for the edge of the plateau, then Sir Hubert, the third engineer, the mess boy, Liavaag and I went on, dragging the other two sledges. The south-westerly breeze began to whip up harsh sand-dry snow against our legs, and we were compelled to stop and fix on our leather leggings.

Nevertheless, the weather was really beautiful, and we continued on our journey heading for the mountain peak as our goal. Ten hours after leaving the ship, at 6 p.m., we stopped and pitched our tent for the night. As our clothing had chafed our necks and as we were a little foot-sore, we melted some snow to obtain water to freshen ourselves. The temperature had dropped to minus 30°C, but the inside of the tent was cosy owing to the little oil heater. We had a cold supper of corned beef, bread, butter, jam, and cheese, after which we cleaned the dishes. The method we employed was effective, if unorthodox; first the plates were heated over the oil burner, then we went outside to rub them over the dry powdered snow, and—hey presto—the dishes were dry and clean.

The tent had a canvas floor and we arranged ourselves on it in our sleeping bags. I lay next to Sir Hubert, and before we fell off to sleep, I asked him why he had chosen Block Bay. I even had wondered how he happened to know of it at all, as it is such a tiny creek. He replied—"I am a citizen of the Antarctic. Don't you remember that I spent three years around Graham's Land in the late 1920s, so you see I have been here before, ski-ing in this very place. I have since then had the feeling of nostalgia about it, and when the plane broke I immediately thought of Block Bay as the best shelter for the ship and," he added smiling, "my chance to revisit this area." He told me that the snow had altered the scenery, and the barrier had changed its shape, but the volcanic mountain which lay head of us remained the same.

Sir Hubert Wilkins was an extremely taciturn man, and therefore on the rare occasions when he did talk, it was always worth listening to him. In many ways, he reminded me of my conception of Jules Verne. As we lay resting in the tent that night for the first time, he mentioned the submarine *Nautilus*, which he had bought for a dollar from the United States Navy, and of his attempt to pierce the ice cap in the Arctic. He had succeeded in sailing below it, but had been unable to carry out his idea of obtaining fresh air by drilling a hole through the ice, because of lack of power in the batteries. Although he had had to abandon the venture, he regarded the attempt he had made as having been worth while, and told us that sometime, someone else, with financial backing, would succeed in carrying out the project. His philosophy was that every person had ideas which appeared crazy to others, and while they might be laughed at and brushed aside at the time, some one else was sure to bring it forth as his own idea, and be given the chance to carry it out.

He was sure that if he had been given government backing—especially if he could have been able to obtain it by dangling the bait of potential power—he could have had all the necessary equipment, and could have achieved a great deal in 1931 as well as piercing the ice cap.

Before he bade us good night and dropped off to sleep, he gave me a piece of advice which should be followed by all aspiring explorers. "Remember, Magnus, you will never gain anything without either personal wealth, or government backing."

I pondered long over his words, and sleep left me. The continual noise of the barrier obtruded in my ears now that I was no longer listening to Sir Hubert's voice. It is a strange phenomena that unless a great upheaval like "calving" of the barrier occurs, the perpetual movement of the ice remains invisible to the eye, although one is always aware of the noises caused by it.

I relived for a few minutes the terrifying experience of the calving of the barrier, and then my mind returned to our departure from Bergen, and I visualized our whole trip, until we "docked" in Block Bay.

I was lying there in the great white wilderness, under the Southern Cross, but not alone, as while Sir Hubert was around there was always such a feeling of security. I raised myself up on my elbow and looked at the great explorer sound asleep, with his face relaxed and at peace. I saw too, by the light of the little petrol lamp, that Liavaag, the third engineer and the mess boy, had already followed the example of the "King of the Antarctic", and I reckoned that there was no reason for me to lie awake.

I think that I must have dropped off to sleep, for I remembered no more until the next morning, 23rd January, when I had to be roused. It was 5 a.m. and our day had begun. We prepared a really good breakfast, consisting of porridge, from melted snow, fishballs, bread, butter and strong coffee. The smell of the coffee warmed our hearts, and we felt inspired to give that little tent an air of gracious living. First we brought in the instruments case to act as a table, placing two anoraks side by side on it to act as a table cloth. The mess boy suggested that we ought to have napkins as well, so I opened the box a little, and brought out some of the paper packing, smoothed it out and laid a little piece at each place. However, the mess boy was told that he was to be our guest; having served us for two years we would now serve him, and he was not allowed even to wash his own dishes, which of course under such circumstances consisted of only a cup, plate, knife, fork, and spoon.

After breakfast was over we struck our tent. We had had only the briefest cat wash that morning, as our water supply only allowed us a handful each to freshen our faces before smearing them over with a cream, the chief ingredient of which was alcohol to act as an anti-freeze. Without this precaution, the breath from our mouths would have encrusted our faces with frost.

Perhaps at this point I ought to explain the method which we employed when dragging the sledges. Each man wore a leather harness to which was fixed a hook, placed so that he took the weight just above the waistline. Attached to this hook was a rope leading to the metal rail of the first sledge, bearing the three petrol drums and the other heavy equipment. The second and lighter sledge was connected to the first and dragged behind it. When dragging, the five of us spread out fan-wise with the man in the centre on a longer rope than the other four. After we had parted company with the ship-based men, the ropes were arranged thus: The leader in the middle dragged on a ten-yard rope, the two at either side of him had eight-yard ropes, while the outside men had six yards. After our night in the tent, Sir Hubert decided that for safety's sake the first man would go out on a fifty-yard rope, so that should he fall into a crevasse, the rest of us would not be dragged with him; it should not be too difficult to drag him back, as we had the weight of the sledges to anchor us.

We exchanged places frequently in order to divide the strain. When it was the turn of Sir Hubert to lead, we Norwegians, accustomed though we were to ski-ing, had to beg him to reduce speed as we could not keep up with him under the strain of pulling the heavy load. His strength was phenomenal. A horse would not have managed so well because the animal's own weight would have impeded its progress. Sir Hubert glided along, apparently unaware of the weight dragging from his shoulders.

It was essential at all times to conserve our strength when out in such severe and dry cold, so we did not speak to each other as we moved, and wore protecting scarves over our mouths and noses to prevent choking. Had we overtaxed ourselves and had got out of breath, the cloth protecting our mouths would have frozen.

Sir Hubert directed us to keep heading towards the volcanic mountain regardless of position, as it was such an easily identified landmark. In fact the plan was that should we find a suitable landing place for the plane, near enough to the rocks and then we should construct the base on them, away from the snow.

We stopped at 11 a.m. for coffee which we boiled over the oil burner, although we did not sit down at all while we drank it and ate our biscuits; these were both unpleasant to taste and impossible to swallow in our dry mouths, so we all—even Sir Hubert—resorted to soaking them in our coffee.

By this time we had travelled so far on the barrier that we had a white haze all around us, and the dark blue sky had disappeared. All we could see ahead was the towering black volcanic rock. Sir Hubert judged that we were three or four hours away from it, and said that it was inadvisable to stop again until we reached it.

The next part of our journey was uneventful, and we reached the rock exactly at 2.30 p.m., very tired with sore shoulders, stiff legs, and aching arms. We were glad to loosen our harnesses and lie down on the warm rocks to stretch and relax our aching limbs. In our exhausted state we had forgotten our previous experiment with the skuas, until a few of those ferocious birds began to hover above us. We therefore had to be on the alert lest they pounced, but in spite of their proximity, we managed to have half an hour of rest. After that we rose to prepare our mid-day meal by opening tins of sausages and pea soup, and a container of deep-frozen mashed potatoes which the steward had cooked previously. We even treated ourselves to a tin of pineapples and, needless to say, the coffee pot was reheated.

These rocks were not quite so hot as those at Cape Adare had been, but I noticed that further up the mountain they appeared to be very dry, as if by constant heat. Sir Hubert very wisely decided that after we set up the base we should stop for the night, instead of attempting the return trip. We began by constructing a stone wall round the petrol drums, and worked on until 6 p.m. when our task was completed. Before settling in for the night we took a little tour of exploration round the area.

We estimated that we had built the base at about 1,500 feet above sea level, and as we climbed towards the top, we reckoned that the mountain was at the most 2,000 feet high. The climb was not steep, and on the way we stopped to examine rocks and stones which attracted our attention. The first we came upon were small granite chips, but as we climbed higher the loose pieces of rock were much larger. Although there was no snow or ice covering them, these bare rocks must at one time have been under ice, and had been brought down and scattered by the action of ancient glaciers.

One rock in particular which attracted us was gleaming, not as silver but like gold, and it must have weighed about 100 lb— (50 kilos). We thought that we had stumbled across a fortune, and decided to carry it back to the ship to sell in America when the expedition was over. We already looked upon ourselves as millionaires! All thoughts of scientific exploration now vanished from our minds as we scrutinized every rock in search of signs of the precious metal. There was still plenty of time before 10 p.m. when we had to contact the ship by radio, operated by hand-driven dynamo. As we approached the top we were surprised to come upon a plateau of sand, on which lay several round pebbles. To our great astonishment, peeping from between them were blue mussel shells, and even oyster shells. In total disbelief, we removed our goggles so that we could examine them more closely, but as soon as we bent to pick them up they disintegrated. Digging our fingers beneath the surface we found others embedded in the sand; these were still in a good state of preservation and could easily be handled without damaging them. These finds indicated that this area had once been under the sea, maybe millions of years ago.

We also found slate-like rocks, and by using them as trowels we dug further into the sand until we came to a thick layer of pebbles. Our tools were totally inadequate for proper digging, so we did not discover the actual depth of the deposit of pebbles, but I had a feeling that we were not far off clay, as the sand between the stones was becoming slightly glutinous.

We were really dumbfounded to find conditions at such a height, particularly in the Antarctic. On reaching the summit we found no sign whatever of a crater, which indicated that this mountain, although having warm volcanic rocks in patches, had never really been a volcano itself, although I wondered at the possibility of its having been a part of Mount Siple (15,000 ft) which once had been a mighty volcano.

We filled our pockets with shells for Sir Hubert Wilkins, as apart from his hobby of collecting them he generally distributed specimens to various museums. When we returned to the base, we descended by a different route to encircle the peak. Several skuas hovered above our heads all the way, although they made no attempt at attacking us. We reached the base at 9 p.m. feeling positively ravenous, but first the transmitter had to be assembled ready to contact the ship at 10 p.m.; Sir Hubert and I attended to that, while the other three men erected the tent and prepared our evening meal. This consisted of noodle soup made with milk, stockfish, tinned potatoes, prunes and coffee. The reason why we had stockfish for our main course is that it is very salty; it is a well-known fact that the human body must have salt at all times, and when one is so far away from civilization diet must be strictly controlled.

At 10 p.m. we contacted the ship. The radio officer must have been standing by for we had his reply at once. We informed him of our location on the mountain side, and that all was well with us; he told us that a party would leave the ship the following morning to meet us with more food, water, and other necessary pieces of equipment, and it was suggested that each party would leave simultaneously at 8 a.m.

After the contact with the ship had been made, we sat round the petrol stove on the warm rocks chatting pleasantly. It was almost too difficult to believe that we were in the Antarctic. It was more like an interlude on a pleasant summer evening fishing trip when the tackle is laid aside to have a picnic and forget the cares of the city life. Even at 11 p.m. on these warm rocks, we loosened our anoraks to let in the air. We had some more coffee, and holding our cups we listened spellbound to Sir Hubert, as he related first his adventures during the 1914–1918 war, when he was a war correspondent, and then recounted his previous experiences in the Antarctic. The time passed so quickly that it was 1 a.m. before we thought of sleep.

This time, on account of the warm rocks there was no need to take the petrol stove into the tent. We were even able to leave the flap open to allow fresh air to circulate.

When nearly ready to depart we decided to leave our precious gold rock behind and pick up up next time. It was a wonderful morning, with plenty of sunshine and without even a slight breeze. As we set out the temperature was above zero, and it was real pleasure to ski unhampered. This time we dragged only the light sledge loaded, while the other was empty; instead of all five having to be harnessed all the way, we took it in turns to drag, two at a time. The air was so clear that the sun reflecting on the ice produced a mirage, like a floating mountain which danced ahead of us as we sped along.

We reckoned that if we could keep up the same pace, we could be back at the base in about six to eight hours, provided that we only took a short break for coffee. There was still no need of a compass as the mountain behind us remained the main landmark while the sun, then in the north, would be our guide until we again sighted the dark blue sky, indicating the open water in which the ship sheltered.

It was easy going and we made good speed. On reaching the plateau, although it had looked absolutely flat, we discovered that we were on a slight decline as we were gliding along without any effort. This explained the tough going which we had experienced in the opposite direction.

We stopped for a coffee break after ski-ing for four hours. To our great surprise, the third engineer produced a half bottle of liqueur! This indeed was an occasion, and rather than spoil the taste of the golden liquid by mixing it with bad coffee, we passed round the bottle from mouth to mouth, to appreciate the delectable flavour to the full. It acted upon us like a tonic for immediately we experienced the feeling of our blood coursing through our veins. In honour of the occasion we all autographed the label of the bottle followed by "Antarctic Barrier 24–1–1935", to record the date.

This happy interlude over, we continued on our way until about 2 p.m. when we spotted a dot of orange in the distance. We knew at once the significance of this; the ship's party had arrived at sledge No. 2 before us, and had hoisted a bamboo pole with an orange coloured flag, both to inform us of their arrival and to guide us to the spot.

It was a full hour later when at last we approached the party from the ship, and were welcomed by the savoury smell of a delicious meal, which had been cooked by the steward on the ship and was then in process of being reheated. We had a really enjoyable picnic there in the warm sunshine, and Sir Hubert gave us the option of camping there for the night or alternatively of returning to the base which we had set up. The four of us grinned at each other. We recognized Sir Hubert's tact, and suggested that he should take the decision, which of course was to break up the party and head once more for the mountain. We had brought our tent back with us in case some untoward mishap should occur, but it was certainly a much wiser course to retrace our ski-tracks with our new load.

At 6 p.m. we fixed on our harnesses once more, and with Sir Hubert in the lead we set off for our mountain base while the ship party took the empty sledge back with them. After dragging for three hours, we stopped again and pitched our tent to sleep for a few hours before continuing on our way. Between one and two in the morning we rose again, and after a warming cup of coffee and a sandwich, we resumed the dragging towards the base. This time we were at an advantage as the sun had not yet risen, so we could proceed without our goggles and without the prospect of becoming overheated and exhausted as we neared the warm volcanic rocks.

We finally reached the base at 7.30 a.m., and were glad to have a good rest for a few hours. After everything was properly stacked in readiness for Mr Ellsworth, should he have need of them later, we took observations for the log book. We found that the position of the base was 76° 40′ S. and 137° 50′ W., and that the height was 1,780 feet, while the top of the mountain was approximately 2,150 feet—rather higher than we had previously guessed.

While Sir Hubert and I had been busy with our compasses and sextants, the mess boy, Liavaag, and the third engineer had gone to retrieve our wonderful gold rock, which we were sure was to make our fortunes. As it took them some time, Sir Hubert decided to contact the ship by radio, and it fell to me to turn the dynamo handle; this is worked on the same system as bicycle pedals, one hand after the other.

After hoisting the orange-coloured flag at the top of a bamboo pole to mark the location of the supply base, we set off at 11.30 a.m. dragging our precious load of gold as well as the tent and navigational instruments.

We first observed the dark blue sky at 6 p.m., and from then onwards we kept a look-out for the ship, although we did not get our first view of it until two hours later. Then we stopped and Sir Hubert gingerly opened the instruments case and withdrew some of the paper packing. I wondered what he was up to, and certainly was not prepared for his throwing petrol over them and setting them alight.

I asked him why he did this. He replied, "I am following the Indians' custom of putting up a smoke signal," and thereupon he added a small blanket to the fire. Last he threw on a handful of snow, and sure enough a great column of smoke and steam rose in the clear air. Much to Sir Hubert's delight, we sat round making appropriate vocal noises as the smoke went up. Laughing, he turned to me and said, "I have saved you the trouble of turning the dynamo wheel for the radio."

I turned to look towards the ship to see if there was any reply from them, and after a few minutes came the answer in the form of a flare rocket. Assured that a look-out would be maintained from the ship, we continued on our way in a leisurely fashion and even had some fun by taking turns of sitting on the sledges, with our skis in front, as we descended the hills. This method of travel gave us a bumpy ride but it was worth the fun.

About 10 p.m. we encountered the guards at the outposts of the penguin camp, and by their loud quackings they warned the community that enemies were on the horizon. However, we did not disturb the birds as we had to make a detour round their territory to keep to the snow for ski-ing, and it was just before 11 p.m. on 25th January that we reboarded the *Wyatt Earp*— mission accomplished.

CHAPTER EIGHTEEN

Bound for Bear Island

We bade farewell to the Block Bay penguins early the following morning, 26th January 1935. I was on duty on the bridge as we left, and I gave them three blasts of the whistle in farewell; they stood looking like a lot of forlorn waiters who had queued up for a parting tip and not received any. Their concerted and irate quackings completely drowned the sound of our little engine.

Our sails were hoisted to a south-westerly wind and when the *Wyatt Earp* sailed clear of the little inlet where she had been moored during the past few days, we discovered that we were in open water. Under those favourable conditions we were able to maintain a speed of 9½ knots and soon we rounded the tip of Marie Byrd's Land into the Wrigley Gulf.

At 10 a.m. we sighted the great volcano, Mount Siple. Although the sky was completely cloudless the mountain top was obscured by the steam which rose from the crater. In previous chapters I have commented on various similarities at the extremities of the northern and southern hemispheres, and here I could liken Mount Siple to the newly-formed island which has been thrust up from the sea bed off the Iceland coast. For size there is no comparison, but maybe in a few thousand years, it too will become a giant volcano. In fact the whole of Iceland itself is composed of volcanic rock which is being forced upwards from the ocean's bed.

During my seven-hour watch, we had sailed close to the coastline, and just before I came off duty at 1 p.m. I spotted thousands of seals basking in the sunshine on the beach, which was completely devoid of the ice and snow. Throughout the whole of our journeyings I had always kept my own private log book, and many of the entries referred to the positions of seal colonies in relationship to the penguin camps. The seals always seemed to establish their headquarters in between two colonies of penguins, thus assuring themselves of a larder at either side, and making the whole existence of those harmless little Adelie penguins an enforced state of constant alert against seal attack.

I went to the mess room for my mid-day meal when I came off duty, and then I retired to my cabin, undressed and fell asleep. When I awoke, the engine was silent and I could hear much shouting—in Norwegian. Wondering what it was all about, I looked through the porthole and saw a whale-catching ship lying alongside. I hastily dressed myself and went out on the deck. I had to smile to myself, for the dialect spoken by the men on this catcher was the same spoken by my compatriots on the *Wyatt Earp*. For once I was the odd man out who had to depend on the others to do the talking, as although I could understand them, they used words and idioms which we are not accustomed to in the eastern part. They informed us that they were attached to a factory ship called the *Suderöy* which was lying quite close to us in a northerly direction. We took the chance of requesting them to contact her to ask if they were willing to sell us fresh meat, vegetables, and water. Back came the answer that they would be delighted to supply us with any-thing we required.

We had to alter course slightly to contact the *Suderöy* and on our way we spotted many whales which had already been harpooned. They had been inflated and flagged for identifica-tion purposes by the various catchers which had killed them, and then had been allowed to drift until their quota had been caught, when they would pull them in together.

At about 9 p.m. we noticed a patch of haze on the horizon. We reckoned that it would be the steam from the great boilers on the factory ship, and we set course straight towards it. Within a very short time we sighted the great black ship itself with a wide white painted deck line, but by that time the putrid smell from the flenching deck would have guided us through a dense fog if necessary. We finally reached the *Suderöy* at 10 p.m.

Like our meeting with the *Tafelberg* on the way from Decep-tion Island we drew alongside with a large whale acting as a buffer between the two ships. Great shouts of glee greeted us as a gangway was lowered for us to come aboard. The old *Fanefjord* was well known to the men from Aalesund who were aboard the factory ship, and they were not only glad to see the old ship again, but proud that she was standing up so well to the Antarctic hazards.

The *Suderöy*'s Captain was at the rail to welcome us aboard; he greeted us in both English and in Norwegian, then invited us all to the midnight meal. The explanation of the odd time of the dinner was that since the work on a factory ship continued for twenty-four hours a day on the shift system, midnight was the time when the 6 p.m. men stopped for their "mid-day" meal.

The Americans and I went straight up to the Captain's saloon, but my compatriots from the Aalesund district were naturally waylaid for a reunion with their friends and neighbours from their home villages. Even when the night steward came to announce that dinner was served, we still had a few stragglers from our party to pick up.

We had a real whalers' dinner. The first course consisted of vegetable soup, after which we had a meat course consisting of steaks from a young fin-back whale with which we savoured fried onions and potatoes. For dessert we had real apples and oranges from the fridge. I should have mentioned that the soup too had been freshly made from frozen vegetables and not from tins. Aboard our little ship such meals were not possible.

Back in the Captain's saloon for coffee our own Captain joined the group, and he himself introduced the subject of his regrettable sickness, and how he felt bad that so much had to be left to me with the aid of Liavaag. The *Suderöy*'s Captain listened sympathetically, and at once generously suggested that our Captain should remain aboard his ship to have proper medical care, as on board they had not only a fully-equipped modern hospital, but it so happened that on this trip they had with them, not an ordinary ship's doctor, but a well-known Norwegian hospital specialist, who had come at his own request to study conditions in the far South.

This opportunity seemed like a godsend, but on comparing notes we found out that we would probably be in port in South America many weeks before the *Suderöy* could return to Norway. However, it was decided that our Captain should return to the factory ship the following morning to have a full examination by the specialist on board. To take full advantage of this wonderful opportunity we thought it best to remain alongside the *Suderöy* for at least another day as we were in no hurry to reach Bear Island.

Next day, during the period when our Captain was being examined by the Norwegian specialist in the presence of our own ship's doctor, I took the opportunity of visiting the laboratory on the *Suderöy*. Here there were several chemists busy at work testing the quality of the oil which had been extracted from the whales in the vicinity.

Ranged round the walls were shelves stacked with small pickling jars, each one of them containing embryos which had been found in the bodies of the female whales, but which had been too small to have been detected before the mothers had been killed. Some of those embryos were only a few inches in length, and at this stage closely resembled the foetus of a human baby. Those, however, which had grown to a foot or more, already had the head formed whale-shaped. The largest specimen on display was about two feet in length. One curious factor was that even at the most elementary embryonic stage it was possible to tell the sex. Among other exhibits preserved for study purposes were whale tumours.*

However, the function of the *Suderöy*'s laboratory was not to collect specimens for museums, but mainly to test the quality of oil. The finest oil was sent for the manufacture of margarine and the basis of other food products, while the second grade was set aside for use in the making of soap and cosmetics.

The residue from the meat boilers was compressed into cartons to be sold as animal foodstuffs, while the oily water left in the separating machines would be discharged when the ship returned to Norway and sold to paper factories for making glue.

The scientists were also engaged on another experiment.

---

* Some years ago, a whaling museum was opened in Tönsberg and one of its rooms is set aside for the display of whale embryos. On a recent visit to it, I noticed that there were several specimens similar to those which had fascinated me on the *Suderöy* so many years ago. In other rooms in the Tönsberg museum, there are examples of whale skeleton which had five "finger" bones at the end of each flipper. During the years of mutation of the species, whale "fingers" had first decreased from five to four, and later to three. The whales killed by the *Suderöy* ships were of the four "finger" era.

I also visited the Sandefjord whaling museum. The curator there had once been captain of a whaling vessel which used to put into Deception Harbour, and it was interesting for us both to compare our recollections of the island. He drew my attention to an old whale skeleton which he had on display, pointing out that it had a pelvis bone exactly like that of a human. It did not appear to fit in with the rest of the skeleton and no one had been able to explain its presence.

They had large sections of the outer skin of the animals soaking in big glass containers, and they were trying to invent a process which would enable manufacturers of rainproof clothing to produce the ideal garments for wet weather. (I understand that their experiments had to be terminated because the garments which had been made from whale skins proved to be much too expensive to produce.)

Up on deck, I saw for the first time a whale tongue. It was from a giant blue whale and weighed nearly five tons. In appearance it was not unlike a monster jellyfish for it had all the colours of the rainbow. It was not discarded but included with the rest of the blubber after flenching.

When I returned to our little ship after my tour of the *Suderöy*'s laboratory, word had already got around that our Captain's illness was not so serious that he had to remain aboard the factory ship for hospital treatment; we therefore planned to give him a royal reception when he returned with our ship's doctor, who was then in conference with the Norwegian specialist regarding the necessary treatment.

When they stepped aboard we were all standing to attention, and as one we greeted Captain Holt by raising our arms in salute as a gesture of respect and gratitude that he was to remain with us. He was very touched and cheered by this.

Apparently the diagnosis was heart strain, and the doctor had been instructed to prevent him from undertaking any more arduous duties. Liavaag and I, however, gladly undertook to share his watches between us, as we all had a feeling of security so long as the Captain was on board and at hand to give advice when necessary. Captain Holt had no fear for himself as he had been to the Antarctic many times before and had every confidence in our doctor. The *Suderöy* hospital had supplemented our medical supplies to ensure that we had everything he required until the *Wyatt Earp* docked in South America.

The Captain of the *Suderöy* had also given orders to his steward to be generous regarding the goods which we had purchased, and in particular to give good measure in essential foods such as fresh fruit and vegetables, as well as the fresh meat and water supply which we had requested. Even our little friends, Piggy and Pussy had not been forgotten. Pussy was given as much whale meat as she could consume for a long time, and Piggy had many banquets in store from the left-overs of the meals on the big ship.

Before the time came for our departure, we were all invited to avail ourselves of the amenities aboard the *Suderöy*, and we each accepted gratefully the luxury of a shower as well as the opportunity to launder our clothes, which dried rapidly in a specially constructed room with circulating hot air.

As usual, before we set off we hung our supply of fresh meat on the rigging. This evoked much laughter from the crew of the big ship, and it was in this atmosphere of merriment that we finally bade our friends on the *Suderöy* "Bon Voyage" and "Good Catching" and our little "chug, chug" engine was restarted and we got under way again.

Our meeting with this little bit of Norway had acted as a tonic on us all and once more we were braced to face the adventures which the Antarctic had in store for us.

Our course was set in a south-easterly direction, but we were not alone, as whale-catching ships were all over the area. We even had to thread our way through whales which had already been killed and flagged with bamboo poles. They looked like a fleet of submarines with periscopes up.

The weather was fine and we had the sails set to a westerly wind. We estimated that with the sails together with the engine we should reach Bear Island in two and a half days.

After one day, we began to wonder if we were approaching the barrier, as we had begun to encounter small icebergs and lumps of ice floating in the water To avoid hitting them, an extra look-out had to be maintained, and because of this it was observed that on nearly every ice floe was a penguin; their black "jackets" being clearly defined against the white background. Their presence confirmed our belief that we were close to the barrier, although we could not possibly be close to Bear Island itself.

The following day we sighted what appeared to be the barrier and we took our position by observations of the sun to find that we were 100 miles from Bear Island. This indicated that what we took to be the barrier was a large flat-topped berg, recently formed by the calving of the barrier. This then, was the explanation of the presence of the ice floes, as drifting bergs are always accompanied by smaller bergs and splinters of ice.

Because of the westerly wind we dared not sail alongside to investigate; instead we decided to circumnavigate it, approaching it from the easterly side. It was exactly like a large island and it took us at least five hours to sail round it before returning to our course.

However, late in the evening we sighted mountain tops and this time we had no doubts that soon we would be approaching the barrier. This we did the following morning, the third day after leaving the *Suderöy*.

As we neared land, luck was with us, for we sailed straight into a sheltering lagoon, and there we moored the ship in preparation for our sojourn on Bear Island.

CHAPTER NINETEEN

Nordenskjöld's House

Although everything indicated that we were at Bear Island—even the height of the mountain corresponded with that recorded by previous explorers—to all appearances we had moored alongside the barrier of the main continent.

Flanking the little cove in which the *Wyatt Earp* was sheltering, the ice was so high that we had to raise our 40-foot gangway to almost a perpendicular position. Even after landing, we could not guess where the original boundaries of the island had been.

We had plenty of time at our disposal, so we headed towards the mountain. There we hoped to gain a vantage point from which perhaps we could see some indication of where ice had formed to cover the sea separating the island from the mainland.

Like all other mountains in Antarctica, this one must have been a volcano for the rocks were of volcanic origin. We climbed to about 1,000 feet, and at that height we encircled the mountain, scanning the horizon in all directions. From west northwards to east, we noted mostly water and icebergs. In the opposite direction there was only a white horizon with snow-covered hills and flat plateaus in between. Because of the height of the barrier, there was no sign whatever of wild life. We wondered if the name given to the island had intended to be Bare Island because of its lack of seals, penguins, or even birds; yet perhaps when the shape of the island has been revealed, it will prove to be in the form of a bear. I do not suppose that anyone will ever find out, but what we did discover were traces of past explorers.

At the foot of the mountain a fireplace had been built, and on it there was still some charred wood. Nearby were wooden boxes and bits broken up ready to be burnt; from the condition of the wood, we decided that it had been left by the Charcot expedition of 1910 as it was not old enough to have been left by Captain Cook's expedition of 1774, and too old to have belonged to the *Norvegia* expedition of 1929.

The area was ideal for the erection of a base. The mountain top would provide a landmark from the air, and the large flat plateau made an excellent runway. We therefore prepared a base similar to that which we had erected near Block Bay, but owing to its close proximity to the ship—it was only half an hour's ski-ing time away—and the fact we had plenty of time to spare, we left double provisions of food and built a stone wall round them to ensure they were well sheltered from future storms.

We spent in all about five days in the vicinity, and during that time the engineers took the opportunity of completely overhauling the ship's engine.

After we had set up the base we inspected the steering mechanism. On modern ships, the steering is operated by a special engine, but the *Wyatt Earp* had the type used by sailing ships of the olden days, when the hand-operated steering wheel was directly connected to the rudder by small wheels and chains. Each link of the chains had to be scrutinized and greased and the wheels oiled from time to time. This was our last opportunity to do so for a considerable time, as there was a long journey ahead of us before we could stop again, and already we felt the keen air of autumn in our noses.

However, we did not set off until we had examined the sails, ropes and rigging as well. Early one morning, satisfied that the whole ship was in perfect order, we pulled in the ropes and chugged out of the lagoon.

We set our course to follow the barrier heading northeastwards towards Peter First Island. Every day we were in contact with ships, all of which reported good fishing weather, but they were all heading for open waters and warmer climates, while our little ship would still be steaming along the barrier for many weeks to come.

With the approach of the Antarctic winter, we decided not to attempt to set up any more bases, as further halts might prove to be too hazardous. After passing Peter First Island* our

---

* On 28th January 1929, Captain Nils Larsen and the crew of the *Norwegia* hoisted the Norwegian flag on Peter First Island, thus claiming it for Norway. Although Captain Bellinghausen had sighted and named the island, he had never landed on it and therefore it had never become Russian territory.

next goal was Good Hope Sound, named by Captain Norden-skjöld while he and his party were imprisoned for three years on an island in the stretch of water between the northern tip of Graham Land, and Joinsville Island. In his memoirs he had noted that at the western end of the strait there were many flat islands which were covered with snow the whole year round. So far, only one of them had been named—Dundee Island. We considered that this island might be a suitable goal when we returned southwards again after wintering in South America, so we decided to investigate the sound, entering it from the western side which had been described so clearly by Nordenskjöld.

The route we were following was practically the same as that which we had taken after leaving Deception Island, but of course in the opposite direction. As before, it was a continuous battle against ice and pack ice, but again we sailed safely through it and during the first week of March we entered Good Hope Sound. Once we were in the strait we found that there was a westerly current, with the water free of ice as far as we could see. Soon we approached islands which could have been those to which Nordenskjöld had referred, although there was the possibility that they might have been large icebergs which were stranded on the land shelf in shallow water.

There was one, however, which was without doubt land, for rising in the midst of it was a mountain with bare rocks; we were excited to sight, in a sheltered position at the foot of the mountain, the house built by Nordenskjöld and his party from what they were able to salvage from their wrecked ship *Antarctica*. Here indeed was a thrill in store for us to investigate the house and its surroundings, where the crew of the ship had managed to survive for three years living mainly on seals and penguins.

We dropped anchor in 15 fathoms of water, and taking one of the lifeboats we took turns rowing ashore, to tie up close to the house. It had been built in the hollow of neighbouring volcanic rocks and hills, so there was no snow in its immediate surround-ings; in fact the ground round about the house was quite warm. Nevertheless, the building, which had been constructed in Swedish style, looked very weather-beaten.

It had been secured against the wind by the ship's wires, led over the roof to long poles which had been sunk deeply into the sand. It was interesting to see that they had even managed to make windows, presumably from some of the ship's skylights, and after all those years some of the frames still held the glass.

Even a flag-pole on the roof remained where probably the ship's Swedish flag had flown; but only the remains of the halyard line lay on the ground. Standing against a gable of the house were two barrels which had held salted herrings, because there was still some residue in one of them.

The outside door was hanging off, and we moved it aside to step in first to a small hallway with a door on each side and one at the end. Entering the left-hand door, we gathered that this had been their living room; there, on the table, we found the Swedish flag almost covering the whole top. But it was so rotten it practically disintegrated when it was touched. Nevertheless we wanted to take it with us to send back to Sweden, and to accomplish this, we covered the whole table top first with paper and then with canvas.

The room opposite had been the sleeping quarters, for it had eight bunks; curiously the bed clothes were still there, as were many of the garments which the men had worn.

The third room had served as the kitchen, and a projecting annexe had been their tool room, in which their carpentry and other tools still lay tidily.

In fact so much had been left behind that we could only conclude that they must have departed in a hurry. We would have liked to have taken such souvenirs as the many books which were on the shelves in the living room, but they were much too rotten even to have handled them.

Outside the house, there was a well-trodden pathway leading to the mountain peak upon which still lay a pile of wood and a barrel of Stockholm tar ready to be ignited as soon as a ship was sighted. But the smoke signal had obviously never been necessary. They were rescued in 1903 by an Argentine expedition which must have, by chance, sailed close to the island and spotted the house.

This epic of survival is surely an example to all explorers who find themselves in a perilous situation. The state of the morale of Nordenskjöld and his party can be summed up in the name which they gave to the water over which they must have kept up a perpetual vigilance—Good Hope Sound.

CHAPTER TWENTY

Good Hope Sound

Our next objective was the northern tip of Graham's Land where five men from Nordenskjöld's party had spent a winter under the most incredibly primitive conditions.

Apparently they had set out in one of the lifeboats which had been brought ashore from the wreck of their ship to go in search for more of the equipment of the *Antarctica*, and particularly to try to find some of the ship's provisions. Unfortunately, a sudden freezing up had overtaken them and they were carried to the northern tip of Graham's Land by drifting ice.

To keep alive, they had upturned their boat and built a protecting stone wall right round it, even piling stones on top, and in there they had existed until the ice in the sound had melted the following spring. In the account of his expedition Nordenskjöld related how, when the snow and ice had disappeared, he and his companions in the wooden house had seen smoke rising from the land at the other side of the strait, and had taken another lifeboat across to investigate, thereby rescuing the stranded members of the party whom they had not expected to see alive again.

Our first glimpse of the shelter gave the impression of a huge pile of stones, but on coming closer to it, we saw that it was in the shape of a boat, and rather reminiscent of the derelict Black House cottages which had once been common in the islands and highlands of Scotland. It was only when we went right up to it that we found the opening, and on crawling into it, there we found the upturned boat laid on a foundation of stones. A shaft of light which penetrated a hole in the roof revealed countless seal skins lining the walls. Beneath the hole we found ashes and a few lumps of coal. Between the outside of the boat and the stones there were hundreds more seal skins which had provided protection and helped to retain heat. But I had to go in again to look at the fireplace.

Where did that coal come from? We had to find that out. Just before leaving the interior of the shelter I noticed on the boat's thwart some carved Roman numerals. A closer examination revealed a calendar marking each day, week and month as it had passed.

I think we were all stunned to see the utterly primitive conditions in which men from a highly civilized country had been compelled to live. They had no dishes or cooking utensils and had existed entirely on seal meat and penguin eggs, cooked on a stone in the open fire. Outside the dwelling lay hundreds of seal skeletons and countless shells of penguin eggs. It was all too unbelievable and too impossible to describe, yet there lay the evidence of the men whose will to live had been stronger than the ferocity of the elements which imprisoned them.

There was one question which stayed uppermost in my mind. What did they do for salt? Many ship-wrecked sailors who otherwise could have been saved, have gone mad and drowned by drinking sea water. These men had obviously kept their heads, and the only answer I could think of, was that they had obtained the salt from the blood of the seals which they had drunk as it spurted from the animals at the moment of slaughter. There was plenty of fresh water due to the melting snow on the volcanic rocks.

Only a few hundred yards away from the shelter we found a huge accumulation of coal lying so close to the surface of the ground that it was possible to dig it up with our bare hands. As we walked on, we discovered big lumps lying all over the place, indicating that within the mountains in the area there must be considerable deposits. But the most exciting find of all was the proof of the past existence of an enormous tropical forest, for we came upon huge fossilized trees, up to over a metre in diameter; they were similar in type to Californian pines (*Sequoia gigantea*). Perhaps millions of years ago, the land forebears of the leviathans of the Antarctic waters, the fin-back whales, had made their homes in that very forest.

Alas, I had to leave without further exploration as time was running out. But we took a last look round the deserted house before reboarding our little ship and pulling up the anchor.

Heading further into the sound we came to Dundee Island. As it was late in the evening when we tied up alongside the barrier, we resolved to delay our exploration until the following morning after breakfast was over, and meantime retired to our cabins for a good night's sleep. Unfortunately, in planning this wise course of action, we had not reckoned on the penguin population of the island, for they had come in their thousands to the edge of the barrier and succeeded in keeping us awake during the whole night with continuous quackings. Whether it was a mass protest against our intrusion or a tumultuous welcome we were unable to discern.

When we awoke the following morning, we found that the temperature had fallen well below freezing point, and a strong south-westerly wind was blowing. But in spite of that, we were determined to carry out our plan to explore the island for a possible take-off base for flight the following summer. Therefore, led by Sir Hubert Wilkins, a group of us went ashore fully clad in our ski-ing outfits, and taking with us a sledge loaded with a tent, provisions, our radio, and other equipment.

We had hardly set out before we found ourselves entirely surrounded by penguins, which for a moment or two completely barred our way. Having halted we observed on looking ahead that the ground rose in a gradual incline, although at first we had not noticed the fact from the barrier. To facilitate the ascent we resumed the trek at an angle, with our backs to the wind which literally pushed us upwards. In fact the wind was so strong that after hoisting a bamboo pole on the sledge to act as a mast, to which we attached one of the canvases as a make-shift sail, and hanging on to the sledge, we were pulled along by the wind in the sail at an incredible speed when we came to flat patches. We most certainly would have provided material for a comic film, for as we glided along thousands of penguins followed in close pursuit, sliding on their stomachs and using their feet as propellers.

It took us nearly two and a half hours to reach the top. To our astonishment, we there beheld a natural runway as the plateau was as flat as could be. We estimated that the height of the hill which we had just ascended was between 600 and 800 feet, while the island itself was about 20 miles in length and 8 miles in breadth. Standing at the edge of the plateau we had a clear, unrestricted view of Joinsville Island. To the west of us we had the Pacific Ocean and to the east the Atlantic Ocean. Although to the southwards everything was white, to the north, east and west, the sky was dark, indicating open water. We could not study the horizon for long through our binoculars as the glasses became frosted from our breath; the blowing, drifting snow stung our faces like sharp needles, and removed the black leather stain from our leggings which soon were bleached back to their natural brown state.

The excitement at finding the ready-made runway, together with the breath-taking scenery enhanced by the cold gleaming sun glittering on it, made us forget for once all about our hot coffee. As there was no natural protection in the area, we erected a windbreak some time later, and sat down to a meal which consisted mainly of corned beef. After we had finished, Sir Hubert produced a bottle of brandy with the words "Well, boys." With those two words we all understood what he meant; our goal had been reached and we could return to the ship to make preparations for setting up a base.

On this island there was only one rocky patch entirely bereft of snow. Here the penguins had their camp and I think it was there that we were confronted by one of the greatest surprises of the whole expedition, for the area was a highly organized fortification against attack by seals.

Had we come across this phenomenon without the presence of the birds, we might have come to the conclusion that it had been constructed by primitive man, as there were wall-lined streets running from north to south intersected by others at right angles running from east to west. At regular intervals behind these walls, stone nests were built, each with its entrance acting as a break in the wall from which protruded the head of a penguin constantly looking from side to side, alert against intruders.

At equally regular intervals, on the street side, were placed sharp stones projecting from the walls between the entrances to the nests, and any seal which had attempted to wriggle along would surely have found itself painfully stuck between them.

When we returned to the ship it was early afternoon, but as we had already settled on the location of the take-off area for the next attempt at the trans-Antarctic flight, we could at last take things easy.

I was particularly delighted to be informed that as I had so far been one of the most hard-working members of the expedition; I was to be relieved of any duties connected with the setting up of the base on the plateau, and while that operation was being carried out, I could regard the time as my own to spend as I wished.

I think Sir Hubert had read my mind as we had been at the penguin camp, and had given me this opportunity to be with my feathered friends and to observe alone their way of living and their organized methods of defence against attack by seals.

In all I spent four days studying that penguin camp before we left Dundee Island on 20th March, hoping to sail right through Good Hope Sound from west to east and on to the Weddell Sea.

CHAPTER TWENTY-ONE

Winter in Montevideo

As we neared the Weddell Sea, we found that the approach was blocked by ice, and we had to turn round and sail in the direction whence we had come. But on 25th March 1935 we were really on our way saying *Au revoir* to Antarctica with our course set for the Falkland Islands.

I was on duty when we left Dundee Island, and looking astern at my country's flag fluttering its goodbye to this unknown and ever-changing world, brought once more the pangs of regret experienced the previous year as we had headed for Dunedin. Yet, by the time the watch was over I began to feel a sense of pleasure at the prospect of some straight-forward navigation, with the compass needle pointing north instead of south. Our endurance had been stretched almost to the limit during the past months, and when I rejoined the others I could not help noticing that already they had changed, and were outwardly relaxed and looking forward to the last sea journey of the winter with real pleasure.

We had great fun throwing overboard our dirty clothes in which still lurked the pests of polar expeditions, the fleas. Our fresh issue inspired us all to have a special clean up, plus the luxury of a shave. In fact the whole ship became like a hive of busy bees at work in cleaning activities, for not only were our persons cleansed, but cabins, messroom and galley were all attacked with great zeal, and the ship was once more spotless.

The notoriously rough passage round Cape Horn treated us kindly as it was particularly mild while we headed for the Falklands. We took advantage of a strong westerly wind to hoist all the sails, and the log showed our speed to be around 8 knots. Having left behind the heavy petrol and oil drums at the various bases, our ship was very light.

By this time our supply of fresh water was getting very low and to conserve it for cooking and drinking purposes, we put out tarpaulins to catch the rain water.

Although we were sailing away from the frozen regions and the climate was becoming warmer daily, it was not all sunshine as we sailed northwards. We still had many storms to ride out before we passed the Falkland Islands, and a long way to go before we came through the Roaring Forties.

About a week before we expected to reach Montevideo Sir Hubert suddenly put a question to us all as we sat in the common room—the corridor. "How many of you are willing to return for a third trip to Antarctica?" He added, "Don't answer now, but think about it and let me know before we drop anchor."

Not one person spoke. Amid the deathly silence, I guessed the answer. Most of them had no intention of returning. It was obvious to me that Sir Hubert realized it as well.

Many times as the engine had chugged along I had imagined it saying, "Never again, never again, never again." But now in the silence as I listened to the wind and the flapping of the sails, I seemed to hear my answer, "You are going back, Magnus."

By this time the little *Wyatt Earp* had become so much of me that it was unthinkable to desert her.

Regarding the preparations for the forthcoming spectacular flight which already had world-wide publicity, I had no interest. I only did my duty, but I lived for this little ship, and the love of the creatures of the frozen South; the penguins, the seals and even the whales. At all costs *I* would return.

As I was on watch that night, I reflected over the events of the past two years. During that time everything seemed to have changed. When I had left Bergen, I was little more than a boy, now I was a man, not only responsible for myself but also for the little ship.

Since the beginning of February, I had been acting as captain on account of Captain Holt's sickness. But while this meant that I was in charge of the navigation of the ship, I always deferred to our Captain's greater experience and sought his advice whenever his state of health permitted. I still looked upon myself as the mate and the older man bore no resentment at the fact that the youngest member of the expedition had stepped into his place.

There was only one occasion when I was compelled to act on my own initiative and without his knowledge. We had run into such a fierce gale that I ordered the ship to be turned round so that the stern took the force of the tempest. If I had not taken this quick decision, the sea would have crushed all the deck's fittings. For five days, we had to maintain this south-easterly course with the weather driving us back in the opposite direction from Montevideo.

During this period of crisis when I went alone into the mess-room for a hasty meal, the Captain came in, and sitting down beside me, patted me on the shoulder saying, "Well done, I would have taken exactly the same decision, and Sir Hubert, too, agrees with your judgement."

In the stress of that storm poor Miss Piggy had been totally neglected, and after I had finished that meal, I filled up my plate with tinned meatballs, and went along to reassure her that I had not entirely forgotten her. I gave her a little scratching behind the ears, and as usual she responded to my display of affection with an amiable grunt and snuggled up to me.

It had been in that moment that the stark fact really penetrated my mind. When we reached Montevideo we would have to get rid of our dear Piggy! By this time her proportions were certainly out of alignment for she was so big and fat that her hind legs could scarcely support her. On the days when the weather had permitted she had continued to do her daily tour of the ship, but as she could no longer manœuvre herself over the threshold, it required at least two of us to assist her. But to me she was still the same dear little pig which had been handed up to me at Dunedin. That she had been intended as emergency rations for us was doubtless, and by this time we had been living off tinned food for weeks. Yet no one breathed the suggestion that we could have had a royal feast of pork chops from Piggy. Even if we had been reduced to starvation, I do not believe that any one of us would have swallowed a piece of her, and certainly the steward would have refused to do the cooking.

Piggy was not the only pig to have travelled in Antarctic regions. It was customary for the whaling ships to carry several pigs with them in case of emergency. But I believe that Piggy had the distinction of being the only pig in the world to have travelled quite so far south.

As I continued my musing over past events, particularly the storm which we had recently come through, I smiled at the thought of confronting the port authorities in Montevideo with a cat and a pig as the ship's only two passengers. Had Piggy been on deck in the height of that storm she would have rolled about like a big football. Puss, too had become rather fat and well past the attractive kitten stage, although not so obese as Piggy. Yet, I believed that it was thanks to those two creatures that we were all still sane on approaching the harbour.

We entered Montevideo in the first week of May, and contrary to what I had anticipated, the port authorities who boarded the ship found nothing to complain about, and made no reference whatever to the animals. We were given an anchorage close to the docks.

As I had expected, by the time the ship was berthed everything changed. Everyone was packing his kitbag in preparation for going home, and what we had all endured together was forgotten. Only the mess boy, the engineer, Liavaag and myself were to remain behind to look after the little ship.

We certainly did not expect to catch another glimpse of the others after they had waved goodbye to us. But a great surprise was in store; most of them had only gone to the local hotel long enough to shop around for some civilized clothing for their respective homeward voyages and before they embarked, they returned to have a last look at the *Wyatt Earp,* so resplendently dressed that we did not recognize our companions of the past two years.

We accompanied them ashore to say the final farewells and so ended our second expedition to the Antarctic.

Sir Hubert did not leave with the others but remained in Montevideo, staying in a hotel until the plane was made ready for despatching to North America for repair.

Including our two pets, Piggy and Pussy, there were six of us still remaining on the ship, but very soon, alas, there would only be five, as poor Piggy had to go. Not one of us could bring himself to the point of broaching the subject with the butcher who had been given the contract of supplying the fresh meat to the ship. One day when he came aboard to deliver our supplies in person, he said that he would very much like it if we had a tour of the district as his guest. Unfortunately, he had not the time to take us in his own car, but he would be only too happy if we would accept his invitation, and he would arrange a car and a driver to give us a whole day's sight-seeing.

We were very happy to accept this invitation for a break away from the ship, and to see the countryside beyond the immediate environs of the harbour. When we returned, to our great surprise things had been happening on the ship during our absence. Everything had been cleaned and tidied, even Piggy had gone. Suspecting that she had landed in the butcher's shop, not one of us ate a pork chop so long as the ship remained in harbour.

I am quite sure that this day's sight-seeing had been at the instigation of Sir Hubert, in order to spare, particularly myself, the agony of handing over Piggy for slaughter.

The boat was not the same without our dear Miss Piggy. Even Pussy had changed. She kept searching endlessly for her friend all over the ship until a boat came alongside with fresh water for us. Puss took the opportunity to take leave of our company when the boat returned to shore, no doubt in order to do a little exploring on her own about the docks of Montevideo. When we went to town we often saw her roaming about, and once she even returned to the *Wyatt Earp* in the rowing boat, but smuggled herself ashore again as soon as the opportunity came her way. At one point she disappeared entirely for a whole month, but we were quite sure that although we had lost sight of her, she always kept one eye on the ship.

One day a floating crane came alongside and took the plane off. After that operation had been completed, Sir Hubert came on board to say *Au revoir*, and as he shook hands with each one of us he pushed some rolled up paper into our right hands. Then while he climbed down the ladder, he called, "Have a good drink on me, boys." To our surprise, the rolled-up paper in our hands proved to be five ten dollar notes. He had given us each 50 dollars! In those days that amount of money would not only have supplied us with the best of wines, but could have fitted us all with new clothing from our skins out to magnificent new suits. It had already been arranged that we could draw as much of our pay as we wished from a shipping company in Montevideo who also paid for the provisions, but this generous gift was from Sir Hubert himself.

Our personal clothes which we had brought from home at the beginning of the expedition had long since gone mouldy, and as the climate in Montevideo was hot, I was glad to buy myself a good supply of summer clothing. My companions followed my example, and after that we were so well dressed we felt that we could even invite royalty aboard at any time.

In fact, we received many invitations to visit the homes of wealthy and important families in Montevideo, but in spite of our new smart outfits we had been away from civilization so long that we were too shy to accept.

Unlike our sojourn in Dunedin, there was really nothing for us to do in preparation for the next voyage to the Antarctic, as it had been arranged that all necessary repairs were to be carried out by the local shipyard. Nevertheless, at all times at least one of us had to be aboard to keep an eye on the ship while the work was carried out.

We arranged to do the daily chores between us on a rota system, a week at a time on cooking, dish-washing, messroom, and corridor cleaning; but each attended to his own cabin.

While it was interesting to visit museums and parks or occasionally to have a night out at a cinema, I enjoyed nothing better than to sit either on deck, or relax on my bunk in the cabin reflecting on the happier moments of our Antarctic wanderings. In particular, I recalled my various sorties on the barrier in the company of the ship's doctor who had now left us for good.

The first humorous occasion was when we had visited Deception Island. We had already guessed that the doctor was engaged on some kind of private research, and I was therefore very curious to know what he intended to do at a camp of Emperor penguins which was just outside of the harbour. While we carried buckets to collect eggs, the doctor carried a leather case which rattled with bottles and metal. As soon as we went ashore at a point just outside the Sewing Machine rock, we were surrounded by hundreds of those giant birds. At once the doctor opened his bag and asked us to grab one of them. The mechanic made the mistake of trying to tackle it alone, for the penguin proved to be the greater wrestler. With one swift movement of its flipper, it threw the mechanic into a complete somersault. Nothing daunted, he went into the attack again after he picked himself up, but seeing the futility of his trying to immobilize one of those giant birds single-handed, I went to his assistance with a lasso. With its flippers bound, the bird could not retaliate. At once the doctor produced a glass tube with a rubber pump on the end of it. After we had forced open the huge beak, a good dose of the doctor's concoction was pumped down the throat. The bird swallowed it tearfully and before many seconds had elapsed, it dropped on to the rocks as drunk as could be.

The penguin standing close by was secured likewise, but only a few drops were needed to make it tipsy. Although it did not fall, it reeled about like an inebriated human being, zigzagging and quacking as happy as could be, regarding us as his best friends.

Bird number 3 had only two drops of this wonder medicine. It was little affected by it, except that when the rope was removed, it waved its flippers about as if it were the king of all emperors and showed signs of preparing for a fight. Penguin number 4 was given a very heavy dose and collapsed on the rocks like an enormous burst baloon. We left this one to slumber while we went exploring the camp and to gather eggs. After about two hours we found penguin number 1 beginning to revive, but number 4 was still "under the influence".

After we had returned to the ship with our buckets full of eggs, we went over to the other side of the bay to visit a colony of seals. It was divided up into several sections, each one consisting of a male surrounded by a herd of females, all sprawling on the hot volcanic rocks. There were also a few elephant seals but not nearly so many as we encountered later at Cape Adare. For this visit, the doctor had taken a long bamboo pole, one end of which he had padded with cotton wool covered with gauze. Opening up his case of medicines, he produced a bottle of chloroform, and poured some on the pad which he stuck in front of a male elephant seal. The big fellow first began to sway and after his head fell forwards his whole body collapsed on the rocks. While the male was anaesthetized the doctor repeated the experiment with a female, but the smaller animal went to sleep immediately. When the huge creature came to, he looked around as if he did not recognize his surroundings, but after a spell in the water, he returned to the rocks in his normal state.

Even on the ship, the doctor, whenever he was not on duty as a seaman, was always brewing up some concoction, either in the galley when the meals were over, or in the ship's "hospital" in the hold. One day he decided to treat us all to a new cough mixture which he had invented. Unfortunately for him, none of us had a cough, but we all obliged by taking a spoonful and declaring that it was so good we wanted another dose. That was his hour of glory on the *Wyatt Earp*. I do not know what his particular line of research was to be when he left us after two years to return to the U.S.A., but I knew when I waved him goodbye, that I would always remember him so long as I lived. He was a real original.

Another time when we had gone to carry out a few experiments with the tiny Adélie penguins, we arrived at a camp when the mothers were busy trying to entice their little fledglings into the water. On this occasion, the doctor had refrained from attempting to induce his intoxicating medicines down their throats.

It was very interesting to watch those little creatures, like human babies, terrified of the water. Their mothers had rather more than cajoling to do, and it was fascinating to observe how practical the birds were. They worked in a team bringing ice lumps close to the rocks on which their colony was constructed. Thereupon the mothers each jumped down on a lump followed by her offspring. Having succeeded in getting the baby so far, the mother caused the ice lump to roll and tilt over and the baby lost its balance and fell in.

This interlude aroused our interest in those little creatures, so both the doctor and myself spent all the time we could, when opportunity presented itself, in studying their way of living. We discovered that like human beings, there were different social levels within each colony. The lowest order had to act as guards against seal attack; these birds were compelled to be the first to jump into the water to find out if there were any seals about. If there were none around, the guards popped up their heads above the surface and quacked the "all clear" signal. But should an enemy be lurking below the surface, the watchmen returned hastily to the ice, but many were caught before they could escape.

It was very interesting to observe the formation which the

birds took up while on an ice floe or close to the water. The guards had to stand spaced out facing the water, and behind them at some distance stood their superiors, packed closely together in a circle. At this safe distance they generally had time to disperse when the guards gave the warning signal of seal approach. However, there were times when whole herds of seals would come ashore at one time, and then the close proximity of the superior penguins to each other impeded their escape, and they too were subjected to attack.

Another pattern of penguin life which had intrigued me was that in the mornings the male penguins went first into the water to feed, after which they took over the duty of guarding the unhatched eggs. Then their mates went into the water for their breakfast, each accompanied by a guard. These guard birds were slightly smaller and inferior to the others and they reminded me somewhat of the worker bees in a hive.

As I mused over these fleeting scenes from the past two years, I realized that there was still much to learn about the penguin way of living, and I looked forward happily to my reunion with those dear little Antarctic friends.

In spite of having so little to do in Montevideo, the time passed very quickly, and by the end of September earnest preparations had begun for the third expedition, and for the return of the few members of the party who had not left for good, as well as for the welcome of those who were coming with us for the first time.

Although I had been asked to continue officially as Captain of the ship, I learned to my surprise and delight that Captain Holt was returning, but only in the capacity of adviser in ice conditions in Antarctica. I could now look forward to my command with confidence.

CHAPTER TWENTY-TWO

Third Attempt

On 30th September 1935 everything was ready for us to depart for our third expedition to the Antarctic.

Most of the crew who had shared the dangers with us during the previous two years had not returned, and the majority of the company were newcomers. In all, including Captain Holt, there were now eighteen of us, five Americans, three Canadians and ten Norwegians.

Mr Bernt Balchen, our brilliant chief pilot, had decided to continue his career and had not returned. He had been replaced by a Canadian airman, Mr Hollick-Kenyon, whose experience had been gained mainly in his native country. His two compatriots were old friends of his, and both were to act as mechanics for the plane as well as reserve pilots as they both had had considerable flying experience in Arctic conditions. One of the new Americans, Jo, was an experienced mechanic as well as an electrician, so there would be plenty of assistance should the *Polar Star* run into trouble again.

The doctor had been replaced by another American who had never before been to sea; like his predecessor he had to sign on as Doctor/Ordinary Seaman. We had the same American radio operator, Lans.

We had a new Norwegian steward, as "the Weather Man" had decided not to return. Since Bjarne, our mess boy, had for this trip been promoted to Ordinary Seaman, we had another young Norwegian to take his place as mess boy. There were now two Liavaags, as the A.B./Mate was now officially Mate for the trip and he had brought along his cousin to act as A.B. There were also two more Norwegian engineers, making three in all.

Puss was the last to return. She had not been seen for some

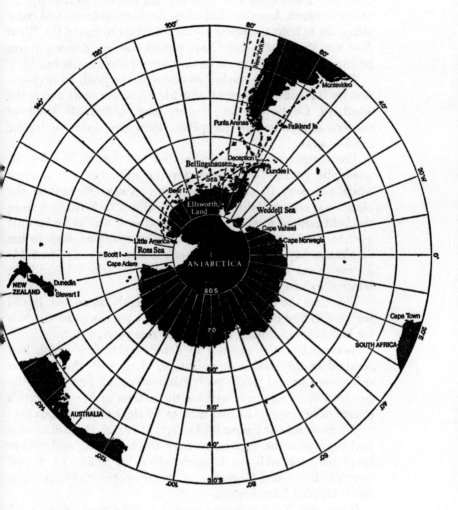

3. 1935–1936 Season

time, and I was quite sure that she had decided to take up her abode in South America. But when the floating crane had come alongside to hoist the plane aboard, the first to board the *Wyatt Earp* was Pussy, who must have sensed that our departure was imminent for she made no further attempt to go ashore.

The *Polar Star* was stacked as before in the hold. In preparation for this coming attempt—for Mr Ellsworth to fly across the Southern Continent—Sir Hubert had added all kinds of modern equipment for the plane, even new spare hydraulic landing gear.

The arrangement for this expedition was that we Norwegians would be entirely responsible for the ship, but would assist when necessary in taking equipment ashore. Regarding the plane, our responsibility would be confined to hoisting it from the hold and on to the barrier, thereafter it was to be handed over to Mr Hollick-Kenyon, his two companions, and Jo the American. My duty as Captain of the ship was too responsible for me to act as relief pilot, the purpose for which I had been selected to join the expedition initially.

This time the team was much more highly organized, but as we were to find out later there was much less camaraderie than we had enjoyed during the previous two years.

Nevertheless, the amount of detailed planning which had resulted in the total reorganization, along with the fact that there were several ready-made bases which we had set up the previous year, augured well for the success of Mr Ellsworth's dream of becoming the first man to fly right across Antarctica.

When we set our course for Deception Island, those of us who had been with the expedition from the beginning and understood only too well the hazards which lay before us, hoped fervently that Good Hope Sound would be open to enable us to reach Dundee Island again.

It was wonderful to listen once more to the music of the wind in the rigging and as the sails flapped, the steady throb of our "chug, chug" engine seemed to repeat the words, "Now all is well, now all is well, now all is well."

The four of us who had remained with the ship in Montevideo welcomed the smells of good Norwegian cooking coming from the galley once more, and after the weeks of relaxation our spirits were high.

The newcomers had to be trained from the beginning regarding their duties aboard. It took some time for them to acquire the art of steering the ship, as well as the hoisting and lowering of the sails but all entered into their new way of living with zest.

One of the Canadians, Pat, had brought a guitar with him and when he was not on duty at the wheel, he sat in the chart room singing and playing hill-billy songs.

The only man who gave the impression of being unable to settle down to his life at sea was the new doctor. Perhaps he had not anticipated the duties involved in his rôle of Ordinary Seaman.

We experienced all kinds of weather on the way to Deception Island, but nevertheless the time seemed to pass quickly, and at the end of October we reached the entrance to Deception Harbour.

Again, we had a great struggle to reach the little pier as the harbour was packed with ice. When we manœuvred to moor the ship, our old friends the Adélie penguins were standing waiting to welcome us ashore.

In spite of the ice in the harbour, as far as we could see the winter had been less severe than usual because there was not so much snow lying, or drifting ice round the islands.

We rested as soon as the engine stopped, for from our past exploration of the whaling station, we knew not only the exact location of fresh water wells but where we could go for a clean up. We therefore headed for the shed where we had previously noticed a boiler for heating water and in a short time we had a good supply of steaming hot water, sufficient to give us all a good bath.

Remembering that the fishing was good round the shores of the harbour, a group of us went out on the ice to try our luck. No skill whatever was needed here, for whenever we put out a line a fish came to the bait, and in a very short time we had sufficient for the meal that evening.

During the time we were fishing my line hooked accidentally on to something in the water. It was fairly open here and looking down I saw what looked like the top of a tree. I called my companions to come over, and together we stared at the curious phenomenon. There was indeed a large area of these living plants, too colossal to be termed seaweed, yet as they were all submerged, the word trees could hardly be their definition. Their tops, like gigantic water-lily leaves, were about two fathoms from the surface of the water, which was so clear we could see the complete shape of the plants. Their rubber-like stems were as thick as a man's body while their branches were as thick as an arm. It was weird to look down and see their stems, which must have been as high as the trunks of jungle trees.

In the Island Magistrate's house their positions were charted and there was a note to the effect that should a ship come close to them, a diver would be required to cut the limbs away from the propeller.

After I returned to Norway, I had the opportunity of discussing this curious seaweed with former whalers, who informed me that it grew around most of the islands, and that it had been noted at some places to attain a height of 200 fathoms. They too remarked on the danger to ship's propellers, adding that the only tool capable of cutting them away was a whale flenching knife.

While on the island I felt compelled to visit the old graveyard. I invited several of my countrymen to come with me and we all had the feeling that the men lying there were pleading to be taken home. That was not possible, but to perpetuate their memories we returned with some paint and repainted the now faded names on the stones, and revived the weather-beaten wooden crosses.

Only when this task was over, I had to scrape away the snow from the spot where I had placed the little Christmas Begonia almost two years before. There I found it, although it was now very frozen, but through the ice, still attached to the stems, gleamed the red flowers.

Our main purpose for returning to Deception Island was to assemble the plane. In preparation for this, one of the trolleys which had been left behind by the whalers was brought down to the beach and a large platform, big enough to hold the *Polar Star*, was constructed on it. Should bad weather then have set in, it would have been possible to move the whole thing into one of the sheds where the task of assembling could have been continued uninterrupted. However, as it turned out, this was not necessary as the weather remained fine during the whole time that we were there, and the mechanics were able to complete the job down at the beach where it was warm.

While the men on shore were building the platform, we on the ship began to make ready the derricks which would hoist the plane from the hold and on to the shore. But first we had to remove the hatch covers to the hold, and as daylight penetrated the compartment which housed the plane, to our surprise and horror, it revealed giant water rats which must have invaded the ship at Montevideo, possibly from barges which had come alongside, or up the anchor chain. However, we had to delay the chasing of the rats until after the plane, its wings, and the other equipment, had been hoisted ashore. During the voyage from Montevideo they had consumed a surprising amount of manila rope and some of the polar equipment. Fortunately the most important items had escaped their jaws, as these had been stored in another compartment, and the separating bulkhead had defeated the teeth of the rodents.

We decided that the best way of getting rid of them was to smoke them out; but before doing so, we removed all the food-stuffs, except those which were in well-sealed tins, and took them up to the deck where they were wrapped in tarpaulins. Taking a trip up to the deserted kitchen at the station, we found a huge soup tureen which we filled with carbide and water. From the bottom of the hold up to the top, we placed a plank to act as a gangway for the rats. Then covering the hatch with tarpaulin, we left an aperture sufficient only for the rats to make their escape. Soon a regiment of rats appeared and made a hasty retreat from the ship and on to the island, where they quickly disappeared.

The invasion of the *Wyatt Earp* by rats from Montevideo solved the mystery of evidence that there had been former rat population on the island. For many years Montevideo had been the last stopping place for whaling ships calling at the island and it was more than likely that each one had brought its own consignment of rats.

I remembered seeing a tin of rat poison when on our last visit to Deception, and a group of us went ashore to find it and more if possible. When we finally succeeded in collecting a sufficient quantity, we spread the poison about the various buildings to prevent their becoming infested and destroyed by OUR rats!

Within a week of our arrival at Deception Island, the mechanics had succeeded in completing their task of assembling the plane, and after the engine had been tested thoroughly, we Norwegians hoisted the *Polar Star*, now complete, on to the hatch and secured it well for the short voyage to Dundee Island. Although the islands were very close to each other, we would be sailing in the region of Hell's Gate where we could expect any kind of weather.

On the way, we would again be passing through the area where Nordenskjöld's ship the *Antarctica* had been screwed down by the ice. While at Deception Island, I had been pondering over possible reasons why the ship had been screwed downwards instead of upwards, as is generally the case when a ship is beset by ice. The only conclusion which I could come to was that the *Antarctica* had not been built especially for Antarctic exploration. It must have served first as a supply ship for the Swedish Navy, and as such, the design of the ship had been entirely different to what was essential for icy waters. Although the *Wyatt Earp* had been reinforced for our expedition, she had originally been a seal catcher, and accordingly had been constructed for Arctic conditions. She was rounded at the waterline and therefore had a greater area for the ice to take a grip and force it upwards. The *Antarctica* must have had sharper lines, allowing the ice to press inwards, thus crushing in her sides at the same time as it had forced the ship downwards.

Our farewell gesture to Deception Island was to pause off the little lighthouse at the entrance to the harbour; there we lit the lamp after filling its large tank to the brim with paraffin. Then we sailed away in the knowledge that should we be unable to leave the Antarctic before the dark days had begun to set in, we had a light to guide us back to safety.

CHAPTER TWENTY-THREE

Antarctic Airfield set up

After passing the lighthouse, we set course for Good Hope Sound.

As I had formed the opinion that the direction of the current had changed since Nordenskjöld's time, I was very anxious to take the opportunity of studying it before we left the area. In order to discover the direction in which it was now flowing, we "shot" the sun with our sextants every four hours during the daytime when the weather permitted. From the positions which we plotted, we discovered that not only was the current flowing westerly (from east to west) but that it was flowing at a speed of about 2 knots. In fact by the application of dead reckoning together with the shooting of the sun, we discovered that we had not progressed as much as we had thought, and that the current had pushed us westwards.

Nevertheless, it was a cheering sign, for now it seemed more than likely that the current in Good Hope Sound would also be westerly and therefore the strait would be free of ice. Another clue as to the direction of the current was that we noticed several large icebergs lying west of Hell's Gate.

By this time we had sailed into a zone which lay between cold and warm air, causing both haze and sleet. With the wings of the *Polar Star* projecting so far from the ship's sides we had to steer with meticulous care. Everyone who was not occupied with esssential duties had to be placed at strategic points to keep a constant look-out whenever we came to snow and haze patches. Should the plane have suffered even the slightest damage, the third attempt at flight would also have had to be abandoned. In this way, we struggled through the pack ice for five days before reaching Good Hope Sound.

Although we spotted several large ice floes near the entrance to the strait, we did not anticipate any difficulty in entering it. But the further we penetrated the sound, the stronger the current appeared to be. Furthermore, we began to notice that the ice floes were breaking up. Soon we were sailing past Nordenskjöld's Island and the sight of his house nestling in the hollow of the volcanic rocks was indeed cheering, for it was a sign that soon we would be approaching Dundee Island.

Very shortly afterwards, however, with Joinsville Island in view, we had to stop and tie the ship alongside a large ice floe. To find out the thickness of the ice on these large floes we used ice drills and discovered that they were at least 10 feet thick, suggesting that the ice was a year old. During the time we were tied alongside the floe, there were constant crackling noises which are heard when the ice is beginning to break up.

Once more we took bearings, but this time from landmarks instead of by shooting the sun, and to our surprise we discovered that we were not standing still, but drifting westwards. This was an indication that farther in the strait the ice had already broken up and was being pushed westwards with the current. It was now necessary for a constant look-out to be kept from the crow's nest to discover large enough spaces between the floes through which we could push our way.

After two days, wide channels were spotted on the north side of the strait and, forcing our way towards them, we continued in a zigzag path as we headed for Dundee Island.

We had, however, to stop about 400 metres from the barrier of Dundee Island to use dynamite. The giant floes ahead of us had come together, and there were several still attached to the barrier itself.

On leaving Deception Island we had begun to make preparations for such a contingency. Long bamboo poles had first been laid out on the deck; then to each of these was attached some twenty sticks of dynamite, arranged round the circumference in four rows with electric wires leading to a battery for operating the detonators.

At this halt there were plenty of cracks into which the poles could be thrust to splinter away the ice and thus form a channel for us to proceed to the barrier. But about 20 metres from the barrier we found that the ice attached to it was so hard-packed that before it was possible to insert the poles we had to prepare holes with our hand-operated ice drills.

We were fortunate here, for with the first firing a great crack appeared at the barrier. Then after attaching the ice anchor to the now separated floe, we towed it sufficiently clear of the barrier to allow the ship to come along side and tie up at the same place where we had been before the winter set in.

With the ship securely moored, we were all very elated that the moment had at long last come to take the *Polar Star* ashore. Indeed, after our arduous voyage from Deception Island, we were all much too excited to take a rest, and even while the steward was busy preparing a meal we had begun the preparations for hoisting the plane on to the island.

When the food was ready, we dispensed with our usual practice of holding three sittings and all ate at one time sitting in the corridor, or on the hatch, with our plates in our hands. Only two hours after the meal had been eaten the plane was safely set on the barrier.

With a feeling of triumph everyone left the ship, and together we dragged the *Polar Star* to the base which had been set up during the time that I had been studying the penguins' way of living.

Those of us who had been with the expedition since its beginning felt a twinge of sadness through our exultation. For here, with the plane safely on Dundee Island, we were experiencing not only the thrill of anticipation but a sense of deflation as well, for we were really at the beginning of the end of the whole expedition.

By this time we who knew Sir Hubert so well could discern his wishes without his giving voice to them. He was obviously anxious that the rest of the equipment should also be brought up at once, while at the same time felt that it was expecting too much of us. But the first engineer, who had been with the ship since Bergen, spoke the words for him. "What about going back for the remainder of the equipment now and cover it up; then we can rest with an easy mind knowing that everything is up here on solid ground?" We all agreed readily, and with the plane and all the equipment left well protected, we returned to the ship thoroughly exhausted.

I was so tired that when I reached my cabin, after removing

only my boots I lay down, otherwise fully clothed, and I was quite sure that everyone else had done likewise. The only sound to be heard was the quacking from my dear little friends, the Adélie penguins.

In spite of my extreme exhaustion, it took a long time before I could sleep. In my mind, I could not help re-experiencing all the hazards which we had endured in order to reach this penultimate stage. All the scattered pieces of the jigsaw puzzle were now coming together, and only a few more pieces had to be inserted in order to complete the picture.

The following morning I awakened early, and looking out of the porthole saw that it was a bright, clear day. As I was still wearing all my clothes, I sat up and leisurely undressed myself. Slipping on my pyjamas, I picked up my wash bucket and went along to the galley to ask the steward for some hot water. He gave me my ration, half a bucketful, and I descended to the engine room to have my "One by Five" standing in comfort beside the diesel engine which supplied the power for the ship. I think that all seaman refer to this wash down, section by section, as "One by Five", and I certainly enjoyed mine that morning after sleeping the whole night in my outer clothes. Feeling refreshed and fully alert, I returned to my cabin where I dressed myself in a complete change of clean clothing.

According to the new rules of the expedition, except for the job of hoisting the scouting plane ashore, the duties of the Norwegians were over for the time being, and I could therefore relax.

I decided to take a leisurely stroll out on deck to ascertain that everything was in order there, and pausing at the doorway to look at the thermometer, discovered that the temperature was 29°C below zero. A biting southerly wind was blowing and I was glad to hear the steward call me to come for my breakfast. The plane group had already eaten and were on the island, presumably busy with their duties of preparation.

About 10 a.m. we had the little scouting plane mounted on its skis and sitting on the barrier. With the strong southerly wind at our backs it was easy for us Norwegians to drag it ourselves up to the base camp without having to call for assistance from the other group.

To our utter astonishment when we reached the base, instead of witnessing a scene of activity, we saw the three plane mechanics cowering under tarpaulins, heating themselves with two of the blowers which were intended to heat the engine of the plane. They excused themselves by muttering something about blistering cold weather. It was not our business to interfere, and we Norwegians returned to the ship to give it a general tidy up.

Early in the afternoon Sir Hubert, who had taken a trip up to the base, returned to the ship and called us together for a conference. He confessed that he had come to the conclusion that the new arrangements had failed already, and that he was appealing to us to return with him to the base to help out after all; from then onwards we were to go back to our old way of working. Those of us who by this time were Antarctic veterans, understood the situation very well. These Canadians, although accustomed to Arctic flying, had now come face to face with the cruel conditions of the Antarctic. The wind had been blowing up the sharp ice needles in their faces and the dry cold air had prevented them from breathing properly. Another thing, they had not yet learned to wear loose clothing and had given priority to maintaining a smart appearance, and therefore were not properly attired for the climatic conditions.

So we readily agreed to give a hand on shore, stating only the conditions that our instructions were to come from Sir Hubert himself and from no one else. Sir Hubert gave his word on that, and called the base crew to the ship to explain everything to them in our presence. They were only too glad to have our help.

Now, working together in a team, our first task was to fill up the tanks of the *Polar Star* with petrol so that it could run up the hill under its own power to the plateau from where it was to take off for the great flight. After the tanks had been filled, we cleaned the wings carefully and then put the "nose tent" on to the plane and set the heaters going to blow heat into the engine. The engine was so cold that it took many hours before it was ready to be started up.

In the meantime our little scouting plane, with Wilkins himself as the pilot, had made two journeys up to the plateau carrying instruments and other light equipment. Then in an attempt at saving us the effort of manhandling the oil drums up to the plateau he stacked them all into the little plane.

As we stood watching it trying to crawl up the slope on full throttle, thick black smoke began to belch out from its rear. Then it began to slide slowly backwards, not straight towards us, but swinging round in a semi-circle as it descended and came to a halt with its nose at the edge of a projection below which was a drop of about fifteen feet. The revving noises which followed suggested that Sir Hubert was making an attempt to take advantage of the little precipice to become airborne.

Instead the plane dropped like a stone and the tail fell off. Nevertheless, it was the most perfect landing that I had ever seen. Sir Hubert was indeed fortunate that the strong wind facing him had come to his assistance, otherwise the tailless plane would have shot straight off the barrier and into the water. That accident both made an end to our little scouting plane and to our last piece of mechanized assistance, as we had already lost the tractor in a crevasse.

No one could help laughing when it was realized that Sir Hubert was unhurt. Even he himself emerged from the wreck in fits of laughter, asking how many metres he had jumped as if he had been giving a ski jumping display. Another man might have been shaken but Sir Hubert regarded the incident as a huge joke.

We returned to the ship to get out our skis and dragging equipment, and assemble the sledges ready to become "sleigh dogs" once more. Meanwhile, the plane crew prepared the *Polar Star* for its run up to the plateau.

Some time later, as we had almost completed our task, we heard to our surprise, the plane engine start up. Looking out towards the base, we saw the first and second flyers climb aboard, where they continued to test the engine. Then after a while we watched them take a few circular turns on the barrier.

Half an hour later it suddenly set off on a straight course, then gathering speed, it took off and roared up into the air. When it came towards the ship, it was like a beautiful big albatross, with the sun shining on its whole body. For a few minutes it continued to encircle the ship while Mr Ellsworth stood gazing at it open-mouthed as if he could not believe his own eyes. In fact, I'm sure that we all had the same reaction while we watched it head for the plateau runway, where it landed, ready for the coming trials and the final take-off. Another piece of my jigsaw picture had slipped into its position.

CHAPTER TWENTY-FOUR

Preparations for the Flight

As soon as the excitement at witnessing the unscheduled flight had died down, feelings of anger against the two impulsive aviators rose.

We had had a very hard day, and were ready for our evening meal and a good rest. The temperature had by this time fallen to 25° below zero Centigrade, which meant that before we could retire to bed we would have to secure the plane and provide it with adequate protection against possible blizzard conditions.

The two sledges had already been bound together with leather thongs in preparation for dragging the equipment up to the plateau the following day; we hastily loaded them with snow anchors to secure the plane, the nose tent, tarpaulins and ropes. In case the plane should be covered over by drifting snow during the night, we added a thick bamboo pole to which was attached a bright orange-coloured flag for marking the position of the *Polar Star*.

Our anxiety to secure the plane as soon as possible did nothing to quell our mounting rancour against these guys, and we deliberately stretched out in the corridor to eat our meal so that we could be together. Taking as long as possible over each course, we rested our bodies and cooled our tempers. This was the first instance of members of the expeditions acting upon their own initiative without permission from the leader, and although he remained silent, it was obvious that Sir Hubert shared our sentiments.

I, as a flyer, well understood the motive behind the impulsive act. The chance to land the plane safely on the plateau in good visibility had been too tempting to miss. But in their exuberance they had given no thought about the work which was to fall on those of us who would have to drag up the laden sledges. They had even left their own skis and snow shoes behind them.

When Sir Hubert at last spoke, he turned to us Norwegians to discuss the situation; after a pause, during which no one spoke, he lifted his left eyebrow in his usual manner of asking for volunteers and said, "Well, boys?"

Four of us rose to follow him. We were joined a few minutes later by the steward who had been preparing hot coffee for our journey and gruel for the two airmen awaiting us on the plateau. Then the six including Sir Hubert and myself set out, dragging the laden sledges.

At first, we were able to use our skis, zigzagging up the more gentle part of the incline, but when it became too steep, we were compelled to change over to snow shoes.

It was exceedingly cold, and up at the plateau it must have been more than 30° below zero Centigrade. Before leaving the ship, I had taken special note of the barometer reading. It had fallen since the morning and although I did not remark on this to anyone, my mind dwelt on it as we were dragging our load. We could expect a change in the weather at any time, and I hoped that at least we could complete our task of mooring and protecting the plane before a storm hit us.

After two hours of arduous dragging, we were still only three-quarters of the way up the hill. Our exhaustion combined with the cold compelled us to stop for a rest and drink a cup of good hot strong coffee. Suddenly, the steward began to imitate the barking of a dog. The rest of us could not help laughing. The situation was really ludicrous. We were all highly skilled and carefully selected men, but that evening we were taking the place of husky dogs all on account of the thoughtlessness of the two flyers, who no doubt by this time were regretting their own piece of showmanship.

The intense cold prevented our sitting for more than two minutes at a time, and even before the cups were half empty we had to get up and move our limbs. After another half an hour of dragging we at last reached the plane, where we were greeted by two very frozen aviators. They had to sip their gruel very slowly before they could even swallow coffee let alone eat solid food.

Without delay we at once anchored the plane, then erected

the nose tent, putting on one of the heaters so that we could thaw ourselves out from time to time as we continued our job of protecting the plane. During those operations, we kept the pilots prisoner inside the warmed nose tent.

With Sir Hubert himself setting the pace of working, after half an hour everything was complete, including the erecting of the marking pole, so we were ready to make the descent to the ship.

As the two airmen were without their skis, I took them and Bjarne for a bobsleigh on the sledges while the other four went on skis. The rapid descent was somewhat bumpy, but at least we were back at the ship in twenty minutes. My first action as I went aboard was to look at the barometer. It was continuing to fall, and I notified Sir Hubert about it. He assured me that he had known about it all day as he had consulted his own private one in his cabin in the morning. He agreed that very soon we could expect a change in the weather.

We were all glad to go to bed, but before leaving for our cabin we were given orders for the following day: morning call at 6 a.m., and breakfast would begin at 6.30 a.m.

When I awakened the following morning, I could not see out of the porthole as it was completely covered by snow. The wind whistled through the vibrating rigging and, being too well acquainted with the signs, my heart sank below the mattress in my bunk. After a brief "cat-wash", I dressed quickly, but before I could reach the door leading to the deck, the news reached me that a blizzard was raging outside. I went out on deck to discover the direction from which the wind was blowing, and found that it was a north-westerly. From this direction of the wind we could console ourselves with the fact that the snow showers would be intermittent; had the wind come from the opposite direction the blizzard would have been continuous. The thermometer reading was 10° below zero Centigrade.

The ship was lying with the port side next to the barrier, and to my consternation when I looked over the starboard side, I saw that the drifting ice had already begun to move towards the ship. Every minute more and more of the open water of our little lagoon was being covered up by it. This was caused by the strength of the wind overcoming the westerly moving current.

My mind flashed back to the screwing of Nordenskjöld's ship, and I hastened to inform Sir Hubert of the situation.

He agreed with me that the signs were ominous, and action would have to be taken as soon as possible with "all hands on deck". The plane was certainly sitting ready up at the plateau, but much had to be done to ensure the safety of each one of us before we could take the remainder of the equipment ashore and up to the plateau. Sir Hubert recalled the fact that when we had visited the island previously it was discovered that the magnetic compass was useless, as the heavy deposits of iron ore deep in the ground had caused the needle to keep swinging out of course. Therefore other measures would have to be taken from which we could follow direction. Sir Hubert accordingly asked me to call the other men to a meeting for the purpose of explaining the procedure to them.

At the meeting, it was agreed by all that the following measures would be carried out.

(1) An electric cable would be taken from the ship and up to the first base on the barrier where a pole would be erected; on this would be a siren facing in the direction of the plane and it would hoot simultaneously with the ship's whistle to guide us back by sound to the ship should blinding conditions envelop us.

(2) Bamboo poles with orange flags attached to them would be set up at intervals from the base up to the plateau to keep us on the right track.

(3) On every second pole a whistle would be attached, although we each carried one.

(4) Should conditions be so bad that we could not even see the poles, we were to attach ourselves to one leading rope with a distance of 50 metres between each man.

(5) At all times we had to carry food and extra clothing in our rucksacks on the ski runs between the base and the ship.

(6) There would be no set times for meals that day, but the steward and mess boy would have food ready at all times, should we have an opportunity to return for it.

After the instructions had been given Sir Hubert sent us along for our breakfast before attempting our labours. It would be possible to work only between the snow showers, so we took advantage of the first clearing at 9 a.m. to start the operations.

The safety precautions carefully arranged by Sir Hubert

stood us in very great stead, and we all felt very reassured as soon as the siren was set up.

Early in the evening our stint had been completed according to plan, with the addition of two drums of petrol dragged up to the plane.

That night we really enjoyed ourselves in the corridor in a relaxed friendly atmosphere, listening to classical music relayed from America, interspersed by Pat singing hill-billy songs to his own accompaniment on the guitar.

The following morning the ship had to be given first priority. The ice had already begun to press against the shore, and we had to act at once to manoeuvre the ship clear of the barrier. Mooring ropes and ice anchors were first taken on to the barrier and placed in such a position that the windlass could come into operation to edge us away, as the ice pressing against the barrier prevented our using the engine.

By noon we had succeeded in moving the ship into a safe position with her bow heading westwards. All possible precautions had to be taken against mishap in the event of the ice screwing us upwards. The great store of diesel oil left behind by the whalers at Deception Island meant that we could spare some of our own stocks for pumping overboard; the reason for this decision was that when the ship was being lifted up we could pump the oil from one side to the other in order to control the listing. We therefore pumped about 5,000 gallons of our diesel oil over the side although at that time there were still no signs that the ship was beginning to list.

It was fortunate that the heavier equipment had already been transported up to the runway, as the ship's new position meant everything had to be carried over the pack ice.

All that day it continued to snow very heavily and a westerly gale was blowing, bringing the visibility down to only a few metres. Nevertheless, we managed to work on with the help of intermittent blasts on the siren which gave us our sense of direction as we carried the equipment from the ship to shore. With the barometer beginning to rise again we knew that there would be a change for the better in the weather, so we delayed taking the remainder of the equipment up to the runway until there was clear visibility.

But before the blizzard had ceased, the ship had begun to

list over to the port side and a steady watch had to be kept up on the instrument indicating the angle at which the ship was lying.

The following morning there was no water coming into the cooling system, as during the night, the ship had been completely screwed out of the water, but although she was starboard heavy owing to the diesel oil that had been pumped into the starboard tank, the *Wyatt Earp* was in the same position. Had we not anticipated the screwing out of the water our situation might have been extremely menacing.

There was still a gale blowing, but the weather had otherwise improved sufficiently to permit a reduction of the members keeping a watch on board. Owing to the presence of Captain Holt, I was free to join the few who were to ascend to the runway to prepare for the official test flight.

It was about 10 a.m. when we set out for the plateau, accompanied by most of the penguins from the colony on the barrier. Reaching the runway early in the afternoon, we discovered that the snow had drifted high up round the plane, but we knew that the job of clearing it away would not be difficult because it was dry and powdery. All we required to do was to get the plane's engine going and its propeller would do the rest. Yet it took us nearly two hours to get the engine sufficiently heated, partly because of the penguins which had followed us all the way. They were curious and eager to inspect our every movement, and at one point they even crowded into the heating tent to see what was going on there. When the engine was finally hot enough to start, the penguins were all round the plane, and the birds which were standing behind it were caught up in the draught from the propeller and blown quite a distance away. Their places were immediately filled by other penguins, which in their turn were also propelled into flight. To my utter surprise I watched the original birds return for another tossing, and wondered as they whirled about flapping their flippers if some primeval instinct made them imagine that they were capable of flight.

Sir Hubert, who seldom laughed, gave in to uncontrollable mirth at the sight of these flying penguins. He even picked them up and threw them into the wind tunnel caused by the propeller. The birds were enchanted by this game and queued up for their turn.

A bit of nonsense always helped us on our way and it was in a spirit of real comradeship and happiness that we finally succeeded in making the plane ready for flight. By evening it was off the ground for the first official test flight.

As Sir Hubert and I stood gazing up at it, the great man turned to me saying, "Tomorrow, Magnus, it is going to be you and me." I could hardly believe my ears. After all our wanderings in the cause of this forthcoming flight, which seemed as if it was never going to take place, *I* was going to have the opportunity of going up in the *Polar Star* with Sir Hubert himself.

My reply was, "Look down at that little black spot. You know, it has been our home for nearly three years instead of nine months!"

"Do you feel let down," he queried, "or do you think that you have gained anything by the expedition?"

I could not help assuring him that for me it had been a great honour to have served under him, one of the Antarctic's greatest explorers. He smiled a little, but said no more.

The pilots who had taken the plane for this flight were Hollick-Kenyon and Jo, the American mechanic. After circling round for about half an hour, they made a really beautiful landing and reported to Sir Hubert that everything was in perfect order.

The blowlamps had to be kept going from then onwards, and so a watch had to be maintained up at the plateau. We had our radio contact with the ship, and by this means sent orders down to the steward to pack provisions which the relieving watch keepers would take up with them; meantime, except for the two mechanics, we set off on our way down to the ship.

Approaching the barrier we observed that a huge ice pillar had been thrust up on the port side of the ship, towering about 5 to 6 feet high above the rails, but fortunately the ship had not moved her position. The barometer reading was still high and we could therefore count on good weather, particularly since the wind had eased to a light breeze.

While we had been up at the runway, the radio-operator had been in touch with various ships in different vicinities, and from all directions the weather reports were good.

At long last conditions were really on our side instead of against us. In my mind's eye, I saw my jigsaw puzzle once more, this time with the whole of the *Polar Star* slipping into its position.

CHAPTER TWENTY-FIVE

The Polar Star *takes off*

During that night the screwing of the ice continued and by the morning the menacing ice pillar had not only thrust further up but had expanded. The situation with the ship was critical, but while we studied this towering ice giant with dismay the activities up at the plateau had to take priority until the *Polar Star* was on its way.

As a large whaling fleet was then at work at the entrance to the Ross Sea, and would no doubt come to the assistance of the ship should anything happen to it. We left a skeleton crew aboard with Captain Holt, while I accompanied Sir Hubert and the others to the plateau to make ready the plane for the flight.

Since its test flight the previous day, watches had been kept to maintain the heat of the plane's engine, so it was not long before the propeller began to revolve, and within half an hour the first mechanic reported to Sir Hubert that the plane was again ready to take off.

Sir Hubert, keeping to his promise of the previous day, grabbed my arm and said, "Come along". I could hardly believe that the chance had come my way to have a trip in the *Polar Star*. As soon as we had climbed into the cockpit, the great plane ski-ed across the runway and soared up into the air in a perfect take-off.

Sir Hubert, who was at the controls, asked me to have my camera ready so that I could take pictures of the ship. He then headed towards the barrier, and circled the ship several times at a height of about 100 to 200 feet to enable me to photograph the *Wyatt Earp* with the snow monolith pressing against its rails.

After I had succeeded in taking a few snaps, we set course for Snow Hill Island which we reached in about twenty minutes flying time. We encircled it at a fairly low altitude, then set our course for the return flight to Dundee Island at a height of 8,000 feet.

During our short flight we could not find anything wrong with the plane. Radio contact with the ship was perfect and indeed, while still in flight, Sir Hubert gave instruction over the radio that Mr Ellsworth's historic flight, with Hollick-Kenyon as pilot, would take place the following day.

Perhaps I can mention here that the plane was fitted with dual control and during the time that Sir Hubert was transmitting he had switched the controls over to me; thus I had the honour of piloting the plane back to the base, although Sir Hubert took over again for the landing to ascertain for himself that the landing gear was in perfect condition.

One major task had still to be undertaken. This was hauling another six large drums of petrol for the plane from the base at the barrier up to the plateau. Leaving only one mechanic in charge of the plane, the rest of us returned to the ship to have a good meal before reassuming the role of husky dogs.

After a good break everyone left the ship except Captain Holt, Mr Ellsworth and Hollick-Kenyon. We divided into two teams of seven men in each team to drag the two sledges, each of which was loaded with three drums of petrol. The going was hard, but we succeeded in reaching the plateau runway in less than two hours. Immediately on arrival, we set to work to refill the plane's tanks with petrol, after which we loaded all the equipment on board, except the personal belongings of the two men who were to make the flight, as both Lincoln Ellsworth and Hollick-Kenyon had insisted on attending to that themselves.

At 9 p.m. the plane was completely ready and while we returned to the ship, Pat and Jo remained with the plane to relieve Lumburner of his watch duties there.

Reboarding the ship, we were greeted by Mr Ellsworth; he was smiling and so excited about his coming flight that he could hardly wait until the following day to climb into the *Polar Star*.

At exactly 10 a.m., the following morning, 21st November 1935, Mr Lincoln Ellsworth and his pilot Mr Hollick-Kenyon, climbed into the plane for the great take-off. The weather was really perfect for this flight from Dundee Island in the Weddell Sea to the American base in the Ross Sea area set up by Rear-Admiral Byrd with his 1929 expedition. This was later expanded and known as Little America.

As the *Polar Star* took off, we breathed a sigh of relief, knowing it was in perfect condition. Then we raced down to the ship on skis and sledges to be in time to hear the first transmissions from the plane on its way, setting a landmark both in the history of aviation and in the story of the Antarctic.

But the eagerly awaited report turned out to be an anti-climax. Kenyon reported that they were then flying over Stefansson Strait, but that as the fuel gauge celluloid had begun to bulge and likely to burst, they had decided to return. Ten and a half hours after the take-off they were back once more on the runway on Dundee Island.

More labouring for us! Once more we had to drag petrol and oil up from the base for refuelling while the mechanics worked to repair the damaged gauge.

Fortunately, the weather promised to remain clear, and except for the mechanics who remained behind to finish their job and to keep the engine warm, we returned to the ship for a brief night's sleep.

Day began for us at 3 a.m. on 22nd November, when we were called for an early breakfast.

Once more we had to tackle the 5-mile uphill track to the plane on skis and snow shoes, but when we arrived we found the *Polar Star* with its grooming complete and again waiting for flight.

Our big beautiful albatross rose into the air at 8.05 a.m.

The *Polar Star* was an all metal, low wing Northrup mono-plane, 31 feet long, and with a wing span of 48 feet. It had a 600 h.p. Wasp motor, giving a cruising range of 5,000 miles at 230 miles per hour, and it could land at less than 50 miles per hour.

The weight of the plane itself was 7,789 pounds, and the amount of petrol required to make the 2,300-mile flight along the Antarctic archipelago and across the Continent to Little America in the Bay of Whales, weighed 2,796 pounds for the anticipated 14 hours' flight.

At 12.22 the plane reported by radio that once again it had crossed Stefansson Strait and had climbed to an altitude of

13,000 feet. Kenyon reported, too, that the temperature reading in the plane was 10°F, and at that moment the plane was already flying over unknown territory.

The next radio contact from the plane was at 4.15 p.m. and the report was that the *Polar Star* had covered 1,000 miles, and they were still 1,300 miles from the Bay of Whales.

There was great consternation on board when, after many more hours passed, the plane failed to contact us again. Judging from the time when they should have made the next contact, we plotted the position where either the transmitter had failed or where they must have landed. This point we reckoned was approximately latitude 79° 12′ S. and longitude 104° 00′ W., with the South Pole 750 miles south of them.

From then onwards, the ship's radio was on all the time and a listening rota was arranged in case Kenyon managed to get through to us again.

We were in a predicament. The ship was stuck in the ice and we were out of contact with the plane. Only one thing could save us, an easterly gale. This could help disperse the westerly-moving ice in which the *Wyatt Earp* was completely encased. We informed New York by radio of our situation, emphasizing that as things were we could do nothing to help Ellsworth and Kenyon.

After a few days, however, the barometer began to fall and faint crackling sounds could be heard coming from the pack ice. On 27th November, the ship began to drift westwards with the moving pack ice. During our period of entrenchment, we kept working frantically in an attempt at tipping over the ice pillar which by this time literally towered above the deck. Had it fallen over the ship it would surely have sliced the *Wyatt Earp* in two.

After many hours of hard work at chipping, followed by the use of ice anchors, snatch blocks and windlass, we finally succeeded in breaking the giant monolith just above the level of the rail and the top part fell over on to the pack ice. By this time, the ship itself was very slowly edging downwards.

Two days later water began to seep into the cooling system once more and the ship straightened. But still the pack ice prevented our starting the engine, although we drifted westwards with the current at a rate of about one and a half to two miles an hour until we again sighted Nordenskjöld's house.

Suddenly, the ice broke, and we came into a small open lake. There we started the engine, and sailed as far as we could towards the island, then moored the ship to the pack ice outside the hut.

Until it was possible for us to proceed further with the ship we went ashore to explore once more the environs of the cabin which had been built from the wreck of Nordenskjöld's ship *Antarctica*. This time we realized that during our previous visit we had been the first humans to set foot on the island since it had been vacated hurriedly more than thirty years before, when the Nordenskjöld expedition had been rescued. Further evidence of the hasty retreat lay with the mummified bodies of white sledge dogs, still lying where they had been shot. Searching around, we also found a pair of ice skates, wooden shoes, some tins of sardines, pepper, salt, and mustard. We even found some cakes of chocolate, still in a fresh condition. Indeed, everything was eatable except for the salted herrings which we noticed on our last visit.

Dr Nils Otto Gustav Nordenskjöld was one of the most daring explorers of the Antarctic. Prior to his party's imprisonment on the island he had been appointed lecturer in geology and mineralogy at Uppsala University; then in 1895–7 he had penetrated into the hitherto unknown interior of Tierra del Fuego. Following his rescue from the Antarctic, he made an expedition to the Andes and penetrated the northern forests of Bolivia. Later, in conjunction with J. Gunnar Anderson, who had been the geologist of his Antarctic expedition, he proved that the Antarctic archipelago must have been the continuation of the South American Andes mountains.

His theory had even been supported by our own observations of the previous year, when we indentified fossilized trees of Californian Sequoia type.

Indeed, the expeditions of our little ship *Wyatt Earp* have also proved to be noteworthy in the history of Antarctic exploration. She was, as far as records show, not only the smallest ship to have braved these perilous waters, but she was handicapped by having to carry for 48,000 miles the *Polar Star* in search of a take-off base for a 12 to 14-hour flight, thus proving that at all times the waters of the Antarctic are unpredictable.

CHAPTER TWENTY-SIX

Search for the Polar Star

During the time that the ship was unable to proceed owing to the pack ice we made the most of our enforced sojourn in the vicinity by once more exploring Nordenskjöld's island.

Among some bare rocks we came across sandy patches in which there were fossils of various forms of crustacea, including oysters, clams, and crayfish, all of which may have lived as many as 100 million years ago. These, together with our previous finding of fossils of the gigantic sequoia trees, were definite proofs that the vast frozen continent must at one time have had a temperate, if not near tropical, climate. We also found many fresh water springs, which must have been a godsend to the marooned party from the ship *Antarctica*.

Although we searched about for ancient human skeletons, we did not find any and indeed I have never heard of any evidence of prehistoric man in the Antarctic Continent. Studying the various faces of the cliff walls, the strata suggested that the level of the sea must have receded during the centuries. We found large blocks of white granite, which must have been brought down from the mountains by the action of the ice and this had also carved giant pot-holes in the rocks by its screwing movements.

Had time allowed, we could have found out much more on this interesting island, but essentially we had to keep close contact with the ship.

Suddenly an east-north-easterly storm began, together with a heavy snowfall, and the ship began to drift along with the ice towards open water. As soon as we reached the open water we set our course for Stefansson Strait and on to the Bellinghausen Sea. Although a constant listening rota had been maintained during all this time, still no word had come from

Ellsworth and Kenyon; we therefore set out in an endeavour to reach the nearest point of the barrier to the location of a possible landing of the plane.

It could only be as the outcome of the greatest skill and good fortune if we succeeded in our objective, because once again we had to enter the greatest iceberg region of the world, and the experience which we had gained during our previous passage gave us no confidence to face the trials ahead of us. Only the newcomers to the expedition were oblivious of the fact that they were approaching a great ice cemetery in which the giant tombstones would not record the location of their burial. But the *Wyatt Earp* had negotiated those treacherous waters before, and we fervently hoped that she would carry us through them safely again. To avoid the great bergs, growlers and heavy seas, we kept our course as close as possible to the barrier until we came to south of Ronne Bay, where we stopped and moored the ship alongside the barrier. Here we made preparations for our first sortie in search of the two missing men.

I was to lead the first search party, and Bjarne, the second engineer, and the steward were selected to accompany me. We had to take a ski journey of 50 miles into the interior to reach the point which we had charted to be the possible location of the plane if it had been forced to land.

Meantime, the mechanics set to work in an endeavour to repair the little scouting plane.

We set out on a bitterly cold day, dragging a sledge on which was stacked a tent, food and other necessary equipment. There was a light wind in our faces and the journey took just over six hours to reach the charted position. We searched over a wide area, but we could find no evidence whatever of the plane having landed. Tired out, we erected the tent to rest for four hours before retracing our tracks to the ship.

While we had been away there had been a radio message from New York informing Sir Hubert that a new Nordrup plane was already on its way from the U.S.A. and we would have to return to Punta Arenas to collect it.

Once more we had to face the terrors of the winding passage through the towering icebergs. But first we had to set course for Deception Island as we were running short of water and also we had to refill our fuel tanks with diesel oil. Our cruising capacity of diesel oil was 11,000 miles and we therefore could not take the risk of running out of fuel, particularly since we knew that there was plenty at Deception.

When we arrived at Punta Arenas, in spite of our perilous journey and stop at Deception, we were there before the ship bringing our relief plane. Every situation can have a funny side to it, and our stay in Magallanes can beyond doubt evoke mirth when viewed in retrospect. In the first place we had arrived without permission and without the aid of a navigational chart, let alone a pilot. To enter the strait, we had to resort to an old school atlas map which someone had brought with him, and by using, this together with the ship's Admiralty sailing direction books, we entered the Magellan Strait at the eastern approach and sailed slowly sough-westwards towards the town of Punta Arenas, capital of the province of Magallanes.

Tying up to a little pier, we were quickly surrounded by an army of soldiers, policemen, and customs officers, who at once boarded our little ship and sealed down all our hatches, allowing us only the minimal daily ration of food while in port. I could not make out whether we were regarded as pirates or spies, but one smiling face in the crowd believed us to be millionaires. He was the ship's chandler, who stood rubbing his hands in anticipation of good business. But it was made only too clear to us that men with European features were far from popular, and the sooner we left, the better.

In a way, I could hardly blame their antagonism, for no information had come from the U.S.A. that we were there to collect a plane; in fact, they had not even heard of our expedition. Although we were permitted to go ashore for necessary purchases, we were warned to keep to the main street only, and to avoid at all cost the narrow side streets where we could expect to be attacked and robbed at any time. Later we found out the reason for those precautions. Once a foreign ship's crew had gone beserk and had entered the town, attacking everyone who came near them; this time the town's authorities were taking no chances.

The natives from these islands west of Tierra del Fuego were small people, a mixture of Indians and Chileans, with skin the colour of red copper.

Whenever we ventured ashore we were always followed by a

policeman, who tapped the edge of the pavement with his baton as a signal to any approaching native that we were to be allowed to pass by in safety.

One day, however, everything changed. A young couple accompanied by an interpreter came to the ship asking to see our doctor. They explained that they had a four-year-old daughter very ill in the town's hospital, and her life was in danger because not only was she suffering from appendicitis as well as the flu, but that the hospital doctor was himself ill from an attack of flu and had declined to operate. The frantic parents begged our ship's doctor to go to the hospital and perform the operation; they had been given written permission both by the hospital authorities and the chief of police to make this request.

Our doctor not only saved that little girl's life, but later performed many other operations while we were in port.

We became popular overnight. Not only did the police insist that the customs officers open up our hatches again, but we were showered with gifts of cakes and flowers from the grateful townspeople. Even the journalists from the local paper came down to the ship for the story, and begged for a photograph of the whole ship's company. It so happened that since Sir Hubert followed his usual custom of refusing to appear on pictures, I was the only one on the photo to have a beard, and because of my distinctive appearance, I was mistaken for the now famous ship's doctor when our names appeared in the paper below the photo.

One evening we were invited ashore as guests of honour to a display of dancing—which proved to be very similar to Scottish Highland dancing. I, presumed to be the man of the occasion, the doctor, was given the only chair as the seat of honour; meanwhile the doctor (perhaps presumed to be only an ordinary seaman) had to share a bench with the others. This mix-up of personalities amused the doctor very much as he preferred to remain *incognito*.

Indeed, the whole situation was hilarious in retrospect. As the evening progressed the local boys, believing the girls to be paying us too much attention, became jealous and threatened to throw us out. Only I was exempt, as the girls had apparently been ignoring me; the reason for this was the prevalence of tuberculosis in the district and the girls had been apprehensive of my studying them too closely lest I chase them up to the hospital for operations.

About ten days after our arrival, the ship carrying our new Nordrup plane arrived, and we left the little pier to tie up alongside the American ship to load on the plane which Lymburner would pilot in search of the *Polar Star*. Returning to the pier, we refilled our tanks with fresh water, and the only meat which we could procure in the town, which was mutton.

As the *Wyatt Earp* slipped her moorings, the little girl whose life had been saved by our doctor stood on the pier with her parents waving us goodbye. Imagine the confusion among the crowd as our doctor stood on deck waving back to her, while I was up on the bridge in charge of the ship as she sailed out into the strait.

We left by the western side of the Magellan Strait, but our progress was greatly impeded by Indians; wearing only G-strings, they surrounded us in their leaking shoddy canoes begging for money and food, and trying to sell their babies to us. The poor little mites were lying almost covered by water in the sodden canoes; so it was little wonder that T.B. was prevalent in the area.

Once clear of the molesting Indians, we were confronted by scenes of real beauty as we sailed past green islands and countless waterfalls. At one point we passed the wreckage of a sailing ship still sticking out of the sand. It had been trapped by the islanders, as so many other craft had been, to get the timber for building their huts. The method of luring the ships off course was to hold up burning torches in the path of an oncoming sailing ship; believing that it was a lighthouse or rock warning, the ship would digress from her course and become stuck in the sand.

Well clear of the Islands, once again we set our course for the Bay of Whales in the Ross Sea.

CHAPTER TWENTY-SEVEN

Rescue of the Fliers

It was now a race against time as we decided to sail direct to the Bay of Whales on the chance that Ellsworth and Kenyon had succeeded in their original objective of flying non-stop to Little America, the station set up by Rear-Admiral Byrd in 1929 when he introduced planes as an aid to exploration in the Antarctic.

There was a north-westerly gale blowing, and we had to set all the sails, not only to gain speed, but in an endeavour to stabilize the ship, which was rolling badly in the mountainous waves. Our log showed that the speed was just over 10 knots. When our little ship began to list heavily we were compelled to dump overboard half of our deck cargo, consisting of drums of oil and petrol, in case the ship became too top heavy and got out of control. After that we began to ride the waves well with an easier motion on the ship.

Back into the iceberg zone we had to battle once more for our dear life. Many times in order to reach open water again, we had to force a passage through pack ice; but we wended our way through towering icebergs in fog and sleet, until on 10th January we became firmly encased in the ice, unable to move an inch.

We could do nothing except wait, and wait, and listen on the radio when we could hear anything; but in the prevailing conditions, the reception was far from clear.

We were in a real predicament. The heavy swell below the ice threatened from time to time to suck us downwards, and we began to fear a downward screwing, such as had been the fate of the ship *Antarctica*. But once more we were thrust upwards. We seemed so near and yet so far from the barrier, for only a mile and a half off on our port side, was the point of King Edward VII Land.

Quite unexpectedly we had radio communication with the British ship *Discovery II* which was in open water west of us, and steaming towards the Bay of Whales in search of our two missing men. The British ship had its own scouting plane, and was therefore able to make the search over Little America without entering the ice patch which imprisoned us.

It was a great relief to hear that radio message, needless to say. We were in the position not only of being unable to put into action our new Nordrup plane, but it seemed likely that if we were entrenched much longer our little ship could be in danger; so on our own behalf, it was good to know that help was at hand.

On 15th January at 10 p.m. we were informed that the pilot of the scouting plane from the *Discovery II* had, while encircling Little America, spotted two specks moving in the snow. Flying at a lower altitude, he realized that the specks were the missing men who were frantically waving up to him.

In case they had not been able to make sufficient use of the vast amenities of Little America, he had dropped a parachute with supplies which included underwear and some outer clothing, as well as food, chocolate and tobacco.

Four days later, on the 19th, *Discovery II* had been able to move close enough to the barrier to send out their launch and bring Ellsworth and Kenyon safely aboard.

Late the following night, as the rays of the setting midnight sun spread over the southern sky, we heard the sad news over the radio that Britain's King George V had passed away at 10 p.m. That was 20th January 1936. In respect we hoisted on the foremast the British Red Ensign at half mast, and on the aftermast, the American flag at half mast, and similarly, our own Norwegian flag at the stern.

Next day the wind veered round, and two days later this allowed us to move a little. On 25th January, we joined up with *Discovery II* in the Bay of Whales. After we had tied up alongside the barrier, the motor launch from the British ship brought Ellsworth and Kenyon aboard.

Then they told us their story. In all, it had taken them 22 days instead of 14 hours to make the journey. The first mishap, as we had suspected, was that their radio transmitter failed; then they had been compelled to land four times because of bad weather. On 15th December 1935, they landed 80 miles north-east of Little America as they had run out of petrol, and they completed the journey to Little America on skis. There they had lived for exactly one month before being discovered.

They were most relieved to see us and regretted the dangers which we had been compelled to pass through on their behalf. They confessed to having feared that the *Wyatt Earp* might have been lost with all of us on board, and it was glad news that the *Discovery II* had managed to make contact with us although we were stranded in the ice.

Next, we had to return to realities, and for the last time salvage and bring aboard the *Polar Star*. Once again it was a journey on skis and snow shoes to reach the place where the plane would, no doubt, by this time be buried in drifting snow.

A group of six set out for Little America comprising Sir Hubert, myself, Pat, Lymburner, Jo and Bjarne.

It took us exactly two and a half hours by ski to reach the base. A strange sight greeted us as we approached. It was like a complete village buried by snow, and it seemed as if only the chimneys and radio aerial poles on the roofs of the houses remained unburied. Tunnelling our way inside, we found all possible equipment necessary for the survival of a community. Briefly it could be likened to a modern version of Deception Island.

I was thrilled to enter the private room of the man whom I had taken up in the little plane in Norway and who had chosen me to join the *Wyatt Earp* expedition as a relief flyer.

Rear-Admiral Byrd's needs had been simple; his room was approximately 15 feet square, and consisted of a bunk, a stove, a chair, and a table. Hanging on the walls, which were covered by ice, we found various scientific instruments, but respectfully refrained from touching anything. We did not take even a tiny piece of wood or a scrap of paper as a souvenir, and when we left the room we locked the door behind us again, believing that we might be the last human visitors to enter the place.

However, we made full use of the cooking facilities. There was a big kitchen with a very efficient coal burning stove. Next to the kitchen was a large storage room where there were several frozen carcases hanging on the walls. Before investigating another larder adjoining the meat store, we cut some big slices of beef which we intended to cook and enjoy before setting out. In the other larder we found tinned luxury foods and even a stock of champagne and other stimulating refreshment. The first bottle of champagne which we picked up was corkless, as the frozen champagne had forced it out. There were several other bottles lying about, and, although the glass was broken, the frozen contents still retained the original shape of the bottle.

We cooked a meal worthy of the reputation of a first class restaurant, and after tidying away the dishes and cooking utensils we set out replete and happy. I wished that it had been possible to inspect the many buildings of the practically buried base; but we had to reach the plane as quickly as possible. However, stimulated by our very good meal and liquid refreshments, we managed to make the 80-mile ski journey in just under six and a half hours.

Perhaps I can digress to describe the snow over which we were able to traverse so quickly. It is quite unlike the snow which falls in sub-arctic or temperate climates; the moisture content is so small that it takes one barrel of snow to make three-quarters of a glass of water when melted. For this reason also, we anticipated that we would not require to expend much energy in the operation of uncovering the plane. From past experience we knew that all we had to do was to expose the nose of the plane and the propeller would do the rest after we had erected the nose tent and heated the engine. In a short time we had erected the nose tent and had the blower going to heat up the engine. Then we proceeded to refill the *Polar Star*'s tanks with petrol for its last short journey in the Antarctic.

After about two hours, the blowers had done their work, and the engine was hot enough to be started. As the propeller swung round and increased its revolutions the snow was soon cleared away from the body of the plane.

We had dragged the large petrol drum on a sledge from the ship to Little America, and then up to the plane, so we planned a joy ride extraordinary for our last trip on the continent of Antarctica.

Knotting together every piece of rope which we had with us, to make a long tow rope, we attached the sledge to the plane and set out for our sleigh ride to the barrier dragged along by the *Polar Star* as it sped across the ice on its giant skis.

However, the trip was not so thrilling as we had hoped, as we had not only to contend with the biting cold, but also with the blast from the propellers in our faces. Lymburner and Pat were the lucky ones in comfort in the plane, but as was his wont, Sir Hubert took the brunt of the ice blast himself, for he sat in the front of the sledge and his broad back acted as a slight wind break for the other three of us.

Late that evening, the *Polar Star* was safely back on the barrier alongside the mooring place of the ship. As the accommodation space in the hold was limited, the other, unused Nordrup had to be hoisted on to the barrier to take up its place alongside the *Polar Star* until the hold was made ready to receive them both the next day.

While we were busy with the task of stacking the two planes, one in the lower hold and the other on the tween deck, we were utterly taken aback and astounded when Ellsworth and Kenyon came over to say goodbye to us. They had decided to take the advantage of a trip on the *Discovery II* to Dunedin in order to return to their respective homes in America and Canada, now that their mission was over. They did not seem to mind our being left behind to face once more the most dangerous sea journey in the world!

But we waved a cheerful goodbye to the officers and crew of the British ship which had befriended us, and once more our siren hooted its three long blasts of farewell while we dipped our Norwegian flag in salute before rehoisting it to its half mast position of mourning for King George V.

After the planes had been well secured in their respective positions in the hold, we dumped overboard the rest of our deck cargo of petrol and oil which was not now required, then we rehoisted the sails and started the engine, to leave the Bay of Whales and set course for Deception Island.

CHAPTER TWENTY-EIGHT

Farewell to Antarctica

Our final struggle northwards through the Ross Sea, Amundsen Sea, and the Bellinghausen Sea up to Graham's Land was far worse than what we had to endure before. But miraculously once more we reached the safety of Deception Island in the middle of March.

The little lighthouse at the entrance to the harbour was blinking its welcome to us, for the lamp which we had lit on leaving after the previous visit was still burning.

Again we tied up alongside our little pier to relax in safety in the precincts of this natural haven, while our dear little friends, the Adélie penguins stood quacking their welcome, and completely surrounded us as we stepped ashore.

After our gruelling journey, our engine had to be thoroughly overhauled before we could set out for New York, where the official termination of our expedition would take place. Then on to Norway for the laying up of our little ship.

We were glad of this opportunity to linger a little on the island which we had come to regard as our Antarctic home. And like everyone else exiled for a spell from home, we set out at once to wander through the now very familiar buildings and to explore again our beloved island.

But to our dismay we found that there had been intruders during our absence. These hooligans, whoever they were, had only one apparent purpose in visiting the deserted whaling station—destruction. They had smashed every hut on the station without even having respect to the hospital, the doors and windows of which were completely destroyed. Every piece of chinaware was left in smithereens, and even "The Town Hall" piano was left minus a keyboard.

I refrain from revealing the brand of cigarettes, the empty

packets of which littered the whole desolate station, but it certainly revealed the probable identity of the invaders.

Those of us who had taken part in the careful repairing of the storm-damaged buildings during the first call of the *Wyatt Earp* at the deserted station felt it as a great blow. This time the buildings were quite beyond repair, and sadly we had to leave the ruins as they were. But I had one consolation, the marauders had not found the old isolated graveyard. I had to see for myself that the graves of my countrymen had not been desecrated. The stones were as we had left them, and digging away the snow at the spot where I had left my Christmas Begonia I found it this time a solid ice lump, through which still gleamed a faint streak of red.

But we could not leave the Antarctic on a sad note. We Norwegians planned a typical Sunday afternoon winter entertainment for the Americans—ski jumping. Only we were not to be the jumpers, but our darling little feathered friends, the penguins.

Therefore at precisely 2 p.m. on a Sunday afternoon, the world's first penguin ski jumping competition began. Ten little Adélies were lined up, and each had a blue number painted on its white chest. As the competition for the championship progressed, it was difficult to decide who was getting the most fun out of it, the Norwegians, the Americans or the penguins. We had built for the occasion a platform on the hillside about 2 feet high, to terminate the slope down which the penguins "skied" on their stomachs prior to their "jump". The penguins appeared to revel in this new sport and kept returning to improve their techniques, quacking their own applause during their jumps. We began to bet on which penguin would become world champion. The longest and most spectacular "flight" was two and a half yards.

After the penguin ski jumping event was over, we continued the day's winter sports by having some fun on our own skis, and in a light-hearted mood, we returned to the ship for some refreshment. As we sat at the table, Sir Hubert and I began to calculate our ski-ing mileage during the whole expedition; we reckoned that the total distance which he and I had skied over the barrier on the continent was well over 600 miles.

It was with the greatest of regret that we decided that the

the time had come to leave Deception Island, as this time it was to be farewell for ever.

We left the little harbour with the still flickering light at its entrance, and dipped our flag in farewell. Later we repeated this gesture to all the living creatures of the Antarctic, the whales, the seals, the petrels, the skuas, and our dear little friends, the penguins.

I was on my way home to Norway and to my old grandfather, who together with his cronies from their sailing days would once more sit round the model of the full-rigged ship on the table in our smoke-filled sitting room. This time they would listen to *my* story, my Saga of the White Horizon.

Index

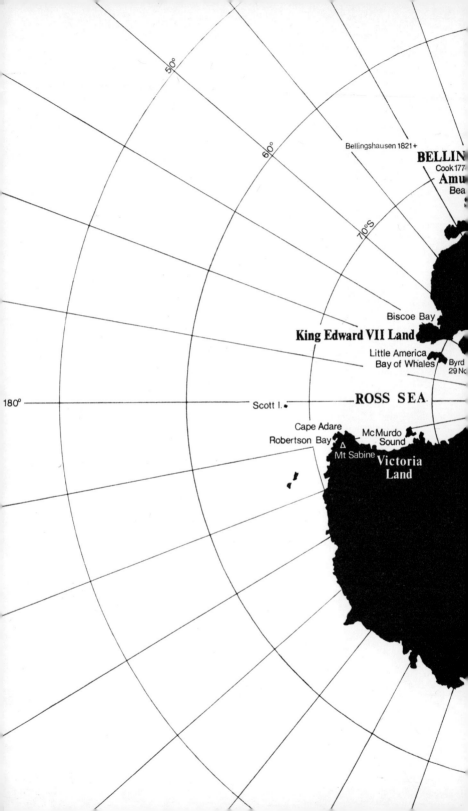